Artist Development Essentials

Artist Development Essentials

The Key to Structuring a Sustainable Profile in the Music Industry

Hristo Penchev

BEP BUSINESS EXPERT PRESS

Artist Development Essentials: The Key to Structuring a Sustainable Profile in the Music Industry
Copyright © Business Expert Press, LLC, 2019.

First published in 2019 by
Business Expert Press, LLC
222 East 46th Street, New York, NY 10017
www.businessexpertpress.com

ISBN-13: 978-1-94819-882-0 (paperback)
ISBN-13: 978-1-94819-883-7 (e-book)

Business Expert Press Sports and Entertainment Management and Marketing Collection

Collection ISSN: 2333-8644 (print)
Collection ISSN: 2333-8652 (electronic)

Cover and interior design by S4Carlisle Publishing Services Private Ltd., Chennai, India

First edition: 2019

10 9 8 7 6 5 4 3 2 1

Printed in the United States of America.

Dedication

I would like to dedicate this book to every artist who has inspired me and guided my development—both personal and professional—through their art. Also, to every person that understands the significance of music and realizes their need to be involved in it. Lastly, I would like to dedicate this book to the music itself, too—for making my life meaningful, for giving it purpose, and for always being there for me, even when no one else has been.

Abstract

As a constantly evolving and developing industry, the music business environment continues to establish new standards in terms of operational efficiency, dynamics between the different parties involved in the professional cycles, and constructing and performing methodologies in the process of achieving the desired results that all the participants in the music world have to adapt to in order to establish a sustainable career.

Hence, the main purpose of this book is to provide practical advice suitable to both aspiring music professionals and artists that need detailed guidance in the process of developing the basis of a fruitful, promising, and sustainable profile, not only in terms of business performance, but psychologically as well.

Keywords

artist development; artist management; entertainment industry; entrepreneurship; independent music; music; music business; music industry; music marketing; music promotion

Contents

Foreword

It was Spring 2006 when I was set to play my final show with my local band called "Graystar." I was going to tell the guys the next day that I would be leaving the band with an uncertain future in site. The only thing I knew was that I wanted to be a professional musician and use the guitar as my passport to travel the world. By the end of the show, I was speaking to the bass player of what I considered to be a real, worldwide, international touring act called LoveHateHero, as I was told that they were in need of a new lead guitar player to write and record on the group's next record. Needless to say, I was *all* in. There was no other option for me. I was going to move from my small suburban town in Upstate New York to the massive city of Los Angeles, California. During my time in this band, we released two full-length records, toured North America over 25 times in a pimped-out city bus, and had seen a good part of the world. This band taught me everything I needed to know about taking a career and business by the horns and navigating through what can be at times grueling music industry. This small dream of mine to be a professional guitar player in a band has now taken me all over the world, and I have played for millions of screaming fans from all over the world. Not only that, I have been able to play on major records as a session guitarist working for A-List producers and artists and to produce my current band's Escape the Fate record with Grammy Award–nominated super-producer Howard Benson. Being a professional in the music industry for about 14 years, I have learned that the only thing that you can do is be prepared. As preparation meets hard work and a little sprinkle of luck tossed in, you can find yourself in the midst of a storm. I have seen people rise to the top quickly, only to come crashing down just as fast. I can tell you right now that arming yourself with the best information out there will help you out in a tremendous way to help you avoid the pitfalls that I have seen so many artists go through. This book was specifically written for *you* and me the artist, the creative, the entrepreneur, and is applicable for every music act looking for success in the music industry. Do you hope to be a famous rock star? Discover the next *big thing*? Or, do you just want to simply work in the complex world of music? Despite what you may have heard, the music business is larger than ever. Music is being created and consumed at a higher rate than ever before. Within this book, you'll be given necessary tools and insight on how to navigate through this world. The author Hristo and I first met while I was touring though the UK with what I consider to be one of my first professional bands, LoveHate-Hero. The funny thing is that he was actually a fan of us, and I remember him tagging me in a guitar cover that was actually quite impressive. We kept in touch through the years as Hristo has always lent a helping hand in providing us with PR opportunities. We eventually became business partners, and I have had the pleasure of actively managing and developing artist careers alongside him for years now. Hristo is one of the most knowledgeable people I know regarding the music business and is always the first person I call when thinking about branding and other strategies related to growing a music career. I am excited to invite you to read *Artist Development Essentials* and grant the opportunity to best arm yourself for your own personal journey into the business of music.

Kevin "Thrasher" Gruft (Artist, Composer, Producer, Manager)

Preface

Everything started with my passion for music, in general. I believe it is quite a relatable thing to say, so I assume that every person who holds this book in hand will understand when I am saying that art and music, in particular, have always been my driving force, my biggest inspiration, and everything I wanted to be related with when it comes to my future and my life. Since the first time I felt the influence and effect that music has on me, I realized and recognized my deepest desire and strongest aim in life—to inspire other people and be able to do that through expressing myself. Realizing the notion behind the concept of music very much changed the way I thought and perceived everything and everyone around me. It is a trivial and banal cliché, but music is the universal language that many of us count on when it comes to their respective integration in the world nowadays, which has been the case with me as well. I quickly realized that, regardless of my development, intentions, and rational ideas, I would never be able to escape the art's influence, and frankly, this is not something that I believe I would be ever fond of doing. For a long time, I believed that the way to achieve my personal goals was through establishing a career as a musician, and I have spent a lot of time trying to achieve this; however, things were just not working out. Although a necessity, I learned the hard way that possessing incredible passion and drive for success is not enough to give you the results you want. Not at all. So, as it usually happens, there was this one day when I discovered the importance of being objective and honest to myself; I carefully and truthfully assessed my capabilities, talents, and intentions to the best of my potential and established the notion that I can achieve my purpose to inspire people not directly through being a musician but being the person that is helping other talented people to do that. Hence, in writing this book I finally found my way to fulfill my purpose and be in a position to influence and help people that might need my assistance to improve their lives and achieve their dreams. My knowledge and expertise is not a result of education; it is a result of dedication and devotion to my beloved objectives. Coming from a small town and a middle-class family where the cultural trends follow an entirely different schedule than the ones in the rest of the world, I spent most of my life dedicating myself and all of my time, passion, and capacity to music, albeit the unfortunate odds for success in this area. This devotion led me from being a teenager astonished by the essence of music, while being in a room full of posters, magazines, instruments, and more, to an industry professional who is now collaborating and working alongside the very artists and people responsible for my love to music. Very quickly and completely surreal, I was able to befriend and be in constant contact with the faces that used to watch me from the walls of my room as posters. Very soon and way earlier than imagined, I was able to fulfill my instinctive dreams, which marked the stage where I realized the significance of the control you have to establish over your way of thinking and acting.

Preparing and presenting this book has provided me with the opportunity to achieve my biggest goal, put my essence in something I truly believe has the potential to inspire and influence other people's lives, to which I am unspeakably thankful. The process of preparing this body of work has been incredibly therapeutic and helpful, as it gave me the chance to not only better understand and perceive my own knowledge and comprehension on the discussed matter but expand it as well. This book presents and contains all of my passion, knowledge, experience, and observations gathered through years of studying, following, and observing every aspect and every detail of the music culture and its development. It is work created and approached not with the sense of necessity and obligation but with the desire and willingness to influence and endorse the people who share the same passion, love, and approach toward the music world but lack the understanding that they might need in order to fully capitalize on it and use it in the process of achieving their most desired results. There is not a single piece of information in this book that has not been personally tested and proven; there is not a sentence that is serving a decorative purpose. Every word is a visual representation of actual experience and proper knowledge, as this book not only is describing my entire know-how and professional essence, but also contains my full personality and unique traits. This is not a book for the people looking for standard occupation; it is a material for people who are ready to dedicate themselves to following their dreams and need the assistance in the process of achieving them. There is a lot more that I would like to share and express, but it is all explained and expressed in the following pages. Please do not perceive this book as a trivial material presented through a usual methodology. It is more than that, at least for me. Its purpose is not just to educate and provide you with necessary information, but to inspire, influence, and give you the moral and emotional support that you might need during your path to success. Although many people are not capable of understanding the divine power and significance of music, we—the people who have received the opportunity to get to know it—have to feel privileged for the talent of experiencing it and for being fortunate enough to participate in its cycle. The beautiful thing about our love for music is the fact that it can never be described in conventional ways with words and only people who share the same passion toward it can understand it, and that is why I would not even try to explain the full spectrum of my opinion on it, since I know (and I count) that every reader who dares to go through the following pages will understand my position, because if you are not able to do so, this book will not be able to help you. However, if you can relate to my thoughts, please continue reading; there is a great chance that the presented content will be able to indisputably reconstruct and modify your life to the level where it can completely meet your wildest dreams and expectations. Just as it did to me.

Acknowledgments

I would like to thank and acknowledge every music industry professional that I have had the chance and opportunity to collaborate with—for developing my understanding, knowledge, and experience needed for the creation of this book. I would also like to acknowledge Kevin Gruft for inspiring my dream to be involved in the music industry as my music idol and then giving me the opportunity to work alongside him, as a business partner and, most importantly, as a friend. Moreover, I would like to thank every single artist that I have the pleasure to represent—none of this would be possible without you. Last, but not the least, I would like to thank my family for providing me the opportunity to pursue my passion and my closest friends for providing me the support needed to do so.

Introduction

As a constantly changing, evolving, and developing industry, the music business environment continues to present and establish new standards and requirements in terms of operational efficiency, dynamics between the different parties involved in the professional cycles, and constructing and performing methodologies in the process of achieving the desired results, which all the participants in the music world have to adapt to in order to establish a sustainable career. Having said that, the role and significance of the artist development aspect nowadays is very different and complex in comparison to the general perceptions that people possess regarding the exact importance of the concept of developing a well-operating brand that has the characteristics and the potential to meet the main key performance objectives in the current, oversaturated state of the music market. The complexity and high volume of information relevant to the process of preparing and launching the professional life of a formation that has not only the features but also the mindset to achieve high-performance results and succeed with the difficult goal of leaving a unique mark in this specific business sphere include the need for constantly evolving personal knowledge in a field that progresses every single minute as well as permanently driven mentality aiming for success. Hence, the main purpose of this book is to provide practical and useful advice, help, and assistance that would be suitable to both aspiring music professionals that are looking to establish successful activity in the fields of the artist development of the music industry and to artists and music acts who experience the need for receiving detailed guidance in the process of developing the bases of a fruitful, promising, and sustainable career in the music industry, in terms of not only business performance but psychological and mental traits. The aforementioned target will be achieved through providing diversified information on varied topics related to the case, presented in a homogeneous, accessible, and practical manner and constructed in the format of providing guidelines in different steps that lead to the completion of developing an artist's profile that is capable of meeting the music industry standards in this day and age.

Artist Development Essentials will aim to attract both music industry professionals looking for insightful and in-depth knowledge and information regarding the activity of nourishing and developing a music act that has the potential to meet the complex music industry standards nowadays and achieve commercial success. This book and its content is applicable to musicians, artists, and formations that are looking for detailed guidance to elevate their talent, mentality, character, and organizational skills to a level where they can independently assess and regulate the evolution of their own profile and career to success.

CHAPTER 1

Intentions and Talents

The trouble with too many people is they believe the realm of truth always lies within their vision.

—Abraham Lincoln

Personal Assessment

The self-evaluation process is one of the most crucial, defining, and essential stages of the development process of every artist. The main prerequisite needed for the establishment of a professional profile that has the potential to achieve and generate success in the music business is the ability to truly perceive and acknowledge the features and characteristics of your intentions, goals, and talents. It is a necessity of significant importance a career path not based on genuine understanding of the aforementioned matters to be avoided. Such an approach can only contribute to constructing a misbalanced mechanism and configuration, which eventually might be in a position to generate positive short-term professional gradation but ultimately would always hinder the prospect of creating a sustainable, stable, and well-operating participation in the music industry cycle. Having said that, every single endeavor in the music industry should be pursued with genuine drive and natural passion, but approached with an analytical mindset. A career in entertainment should not be perceived as an occupational option, a source of stable income, and an opportunity for constant professional development, leading to a conventional life, but as a passion project. It is the ultimate mistake to pursue only professional growth and success in your respective endeavors, as an artist should be confident in the desire to get involved in the cycle of developing a profile in the entertainment sphere due to being attracted to participating in the process of achieving it. Chasing evanescent goals does not bring the positive results you want, regardless of their nature.

Talent

Ultimately, success in the music industry is a matter of approach, not practice, and it depends on two incredibly simple and comprehensive components, which—if understood, distinguished, and approached with the correct dose of mentality—can build the fundaments of a stable activity in the entertainment business:

- The talent and the ability to produce a high-quality product
- The talent and the ability to showcase and present the talent and ability to produce a high-quality product

Talent is luck. Skill is a result of talent, and ability is a product of effort, determination, and hard work. People are not capable of creating, a characteristic feature that they do not already possess. But they are in a position to drastically improve, evolve, and modify their existing unique traits. Singing well is not a talent; neither is playing in an exceptional manner. These are skills developed through utilizing a talent. Being able or having the desire to express your feelings through ability is a talent. Having the opportunity to see beauty in negative spaces is one as well. Possessing the relentless desire to tackle obstacles in the process of approaching your desires is one, too. That said, an artist should be aware of the clear meaning and characteristics of their potential talents in order to accurately identify them and carefully direct their development in the right direction. The ability to cherish a talent, understand its strengths, and carefully assess the quality of work and results that it can generate objectively is essential for an artist's creative state of mind and thus for the long-term performance of their work.

A note that is important to be recognized and realized as early as possible is the fact that, contrary to the majority of people's expectations and notions, one's talent might not necessarily be related to what one thinks one's biggest passion is. Hence, you need to first very well understand and get to know yourself, as a personality, before encouraging professional development in a certain area. Your talent might not be the one you want, initially, and this does not mean that there is a misconnection between what you want to do and what you can do best, but it indicates that you probably have the wrong idea and misconception of what you truly want to do and how you should execute your plans to do it. Remember to always invest your time and efforts in the activities that you are good at. Many people tend to falsely associate their talents with roles that they think are most compatible with them, but that does not correspond with reality. The mere fact that your passion is music does not mean that you are meant to succeed in your endeavor in this field assuming the role of a musician, for example. Your personal traits might be more suitable to the positions of a manager, booking agent, PR consultant, sound engineer, producer, and so on. This is why it is crucial to avoid dedicating yourself to the urge of committing yourself to the first, instinctive impression you get in terms of clarifying your most desired role and goal. Be receptive and cognizant toward your own profile and capabilities and open to the idea of pursuing and approaching their most suitable and rational application, until you find it. Most of the time, people do not succeed in what they do because they have falsely developed an idea for their development that is not related to the reality of their circumstances, which leads to frustration and desperation caused by the investment of a great amount of time, passion, and effort in an activity that is simply not the right one for them and that, fundamentally, does not provide positive final results. So, if you want to utilize your qualities to their full potential, find their best application, and be sure that you are not confusing it with your own perceptions and ideas of it.

Vision

Possessing the vision to picture yourself and your success in a palpable way is the first sign that you actually own the genuine desire to be involved in the entertainment industry and that it already provides you with one of the main things that you would need in order to establish a successful profile in it—a desired final destination. Success is always a result of imagination, as you can never reach a goal that you are not capable of envisioning. Being a visionary and possessing a significant talent, most certainly, are essential and significant qualities for the establishment of a successful career; however, many artists who are, understandably, relying mainly on their excitement and enthusiasm to progress further with their music industry endeavors tend to neglect the importance of the procedure of bringing their ideas, plans, and notions to life through work. The prospect of creating and achieving a high standard of living by exploiting your personal talents is undoubtedly an extremely attractive perception, that is, however, very difficult and challenging to perform and execute properly. Having said that, an artist should know that imagination is just not enough to achieve results; it is pivotal to have the quality and the ability to bring your imagination to life through hard work and determination. Imagining and picturing your progress will not materialize it. Success does not come by objectifying your thoughts and perceptions of it. Rather, it comes once you develop and shape the said notions of the specific goal that will grant you success, upon completion. It is not about picturing and imagining the results and the consequences of your desired success, but the circumstances and the exact activity that will deliver it to you. It is writing, discussing, gathering opinions, researching, developing a strategic plan of action based on information, conclusions, assumptions and knowledge, testing, modifying, performing, failing, pivoting, perfecting, and never quitting that will transform your ideas, eventually, into reality. So do not let yourself minimize the importance and difficulty of the process of pursuing your desired goals and what exactly that entails.

You should very carefully consider and establish the concrete mission and vision of your career and avoid a significant disunion between your music, your general vision, and your overall presence as an artist to the point where there is no intuitive relationship between the different aspects of your brand. The main priority should always be to aim to develop one homogeneous product, containing image and statement that should be standing out to a point where it can embody and showcase the content of your music through your presence. Or, in other words, you should combine your activities, plans, and projects in such a way as to develop your own, distinguishable style. What do you want to do? Why do you want to do it? How do you want to do it? What would you like to achieve with it? Decide for good what sort and genre of music you want to play. What sort of messages would you like your songs to entail? What type of tracks do you want your group to be related with? Do you want to be an underground band? Do you want to be a pop act? What sort of audience you see yourself attracting—teenagers, adults, or both? What sort of outlets would you like your music to be reviewed by? Consider your image. Think about how you would like people to perceive you as a musician. Think about how you see yourself on stage. Is the notion in your mind compatible with the music you want to play? You should ensure that all of the aforementioned topics form a homogeneous, cohesive product so that every part of your activity can logically relate to the others.

Goals Clarification

Career in the music business should not be the main priority and goal to concentrate on in your life—it should be the only one. Prioritizing your professional development above anything else in your life is necessary if you want to progress to the highest level of your professional aims. It is important to possess the tunnel vision for success in the music world and apply an incredible amount of tenacity to it. You always have to ensure that the goals you have in your mind and the operations that are meant to be completed in order to accomplish these goals would require you to constantly improve yourself and, ultimately, be better than you currently are.

The process of goal clarification is pivotal not only for the purpose of actually achieving your plans but also because the way you approach your activity would form you as an individual and a professional. This is, to a certain extent, the long-term goal, which exceeds the importance of your short-term ones, and it can actually grant you the success that you doubtlessly want to achieve.

Carefully and precisely consider the approach that you would be utilizing in the process of developing your professional activity and career. Think about concrete goals that you want to achieve, the specific numbers that you want to generate with your sales, the size of the audience that you want to attract to your shows, and the duration of your activity that you would like to reach. Now multiply everything by 10. Set goals that are beyond your imagination and expectations; aim to get the results and the accomplishments that are beyond your wildest thoughts. If you put a limit on what you can do and on your belief in yourself, in general, you are placing a ceiling on your potential success. Do not instill borders for your talent. If you do, destroy them. You should have expectations for yourself if you want to achieve the stature that you are aiming for and take advantage of the power of your intention. Constructing and placing high standards and ambitions is one of the most crucial principles that has a direct and undeniable effect on your mentality and build a creative, unique, and innovative state of mind, which, essentially, shapes your mindset to the level that you need to possess in order to be in a position to pursue sustainable and profitable professional longevity in the entertainment industry. By aiming to accomplish unusually and unexpectedly high goals, you will remove and erase all of the unnecessary psychological limitations that your mind has inserted in your perceptions. Once this happens, you will be able to naturally unlock the full capacity of your potential, talent, and ability in order to meet the objectives you have placed for yourself. Unconventional aims require unconventional methodologies in order to be completed, so by putting yourself in a situation where you have to pursue arduous and demanding projects, you will have to automatically and indisputably change your operational behavior and your way of thinking and strategizing in order to do so. Your results will always be only as good as the standards that you are establishing for yourself and that you are aiming to reach. Everything is possible, until it is not. Placing a limit to your expectations, dreams, and desires, essentially, means that you are putting a limit to your own development and success and removing a significant amount of opportunities for professional growth, which is the opposite of what a formation should be working toward at any point of its career. In an endeavor where success is strongly based on belief and trust in your capabilities and qualities, it is of significant importance to avoid a thought process of mentally undermining and underestimating your chances of succeeding in whatever the situation might be. This mentality and approach is not a momentum solution, not a method to be adopted in certain cases and situations. This has to be a monumental part of your vision, understanding, and philosophy for success that you have to completely dedicate yourself to. You have to genuinely believe in the idea of performing and investing yourself into completing ideas that the majority of the people around you would find ridiculous. You have to reinvent your imagination and mind in order to absolutely and fundamentally change your operational behavior. Essentially, the goals that are in place to establish the highest level of incentive for their respective owners are the ones that possess very clear and specific aims and that can be completed within a conceivable and reasonable period; so an artist liking to be efficient and truly successful should always be able to find the right motivation for performing his or her professional duties, regardless of the specifics of their ideas thereof. Additionally, the process of strategizing the fulfillment of your planned activities should be based on and formulated in accordance with either your personal manner of conducting your actions or the eventual results that you are focusing on. Usually, the majority of people find the former option for the more suitable and the more demanding one, considering the need for the person's specific traits to be adjusted and exploited to the defined task's characteristics. Due to this fact, behaviorally formed goals provide the user with a very cohesive methodology and with the opportunity to exercise strong control on the relevant processes, and this produces a more appropriate and convenient environment for approaching long-term goals. Formulating your action plan entirely on the results that you would like to generate is an efficient strategy, which is a very suitable one in the process of completing concrete short-term goals. The exact method of constructing your activity in this area, however, should be based on your personal preferences and unique characteristic qualities. The main thing that should be remembered is that the most crucial and essential part of accomplishing your goals is clearly defining them. Once you have your aims distinctly outlined, you will be able to naturally deduct what the best course of action related to the presented case would be.

Understanding the Music Industry Cycle and Culture

The music industry is not a large amount of money that you would be able to generate while you sleep and spend on fast cars and expensive alcohol. The music industry is not getting attention from all over the world and being recognized as a significant culture figure. The music industry is a narcotic. It is frustration, desperation, devastation. It is an unfair platform that will take your everything and, in exchange, provide you with a minimal chance of achieving your biggest desires, and this is a piece of information that should be properly and very diligently perceived before any activity in this sphere is established, because if you do not think that you are able to not only undergo the said specifics but also overcome the obstacles that they might create, you are not ready and capable of establishing a successful career in this industry. In essence, establishing a professional activity in the music sphere is not something that you necessarily need to want, but rather something that you need to do. An artist would never achieve any level of success if success were the main desired goal.

Arguably, the starting stage for a career in the music industry, where the artist should get familiar and used to the respective working cycle, is one of the most challenging and requiring phases related to the business and marks the first breaking point for many enthusiasts looking to establish activity in this business. Considering the fact that an artist at that early stage of development is still not capable of investing the full potential of their emotional and physical capacity into their professional development, it is of crucial importance for every individual to recognize the significance of being capable of approaching and treating every aspect related to career progress with utmost attention and concentration. In the process of developing a successful product in the music environment, the first point of every aspect of your activity should be related to your approach toward the respective sphere. Hence, an exquisite level of background knowledge about the music industry, the tendencies affecting it, the different roles operating in it, and the dynamics between them is needed before a career in this business is even considered. The correct utilization of your qualities requires strong theoretical and practical knowledge, combined with an intuitive approach to your specific field of action in order to ensure a synchronized attempt for conventional success. Correlation does not imply causation, so you have to be knowledgeable and well informed of the specifics of the operations that you are undertaking and the fixed relationship between them. Natural understanding of the music industry processes is a useful skill to base your professional efforts on at the beginning of your career, but in the long term you cannot afford to rely your activities and career on certain consequences of actions that you have noticed are the source of providing positive results, but you do not know why and how these are actually being generated. You have to understand and know the game that you will need to play. To be aware of the meaning and the structure of the processes that you want to be involved in, include every single detail and characteristic that defines them, since otherwise you will never be able to construct a logical, well-performing activity. You cannot afford to do things without knowing why and how you need to do them or invest yourself in projects and methodologies that you do not understand and just hope for the best results and outcomes. Imagine that you are driving your car and it suddenly breaks down in the middle of the road. You would never just change your tire, get back in it, and try to continue your journey, hoping for the best possible outcome. You would first try to assess and understand the source of the problem, what action would resolve it, and how you should perform that action and then apply all of the acquired knowledge to the situation. Many professionals tend to follow palpable concepts and methodologies for development without being aware of their exact meaning and significance, without having the proper knowledge and experience to do so, and before progressing any further with the establishment of their professional activity—you should be sure that you are not adopting this kind of mentality and approach.

Another big and very naïve misconception among the inexperienced and inept participants in the music industry cycle is the general approach of advancing a career. Such musicians very often and erroneously tend to follow the natural instinct of approaching the procedure of seeking relevant chances and opportunities for brand expansion, without properly understanding the significance of their particular role in this cycle, which is formed around the following three main links and the interconnections between them: industry–artist–audience. The main and general activity frame of the music industry cycle is revolving around these three fundamental components, the relationship between them, and the way that every artist is utilizing their own characteristics in the process of exploiting the already developed tendencies and practices of the said elements to their benefit. The essential notion that should be remembered when it comes to defining your own place and significance in this already established relationship is that—regardless of what part of this professional chain your specific is related to—your main goal with your activity is to create a connection between the other two segments rather than necessarily working toward improving your own standing. The music industry performance is cycle based; that is, the efficiency and success of your career depend on how well you operate in its overall working environment, as success—specifically for an artist—is not possible if your career is not part of a well-operating professional circuit involving the other two aspects. If you are an artist, the best way to add value to your brand and generate interest in your career is by showing your potential and capacity to connect the industry to the general audience. By doing this, you will showcase your ability to be in charge of a brand that can work in the current landscape of the music business and adjust to its specifics, as this will, most certainly, make both the industry and the audience willing to provide you with a platform for career growth.

Connecting with the Industry

Music industry participants do not offer and present opportunities to acts based on their individual opinions of whether they personally enjoy or appreciate the artist's talents. They base their decisions on whether they believe and notice the eventual possibility for achieving rational business success by cooperating with you. You will never receive an opportunity because you are part of a great band that creates amazing music. You will receive a chance for growth if you are capable of generating results that would be beneficial for whoever decides to work with you. Most of the time, music industry professionals do not know what they are looking for until they find it as well. Hence, it is a very wrong strategy to base your development on fulfilling steps and developing yourself to a form that you believe the music industry wants and seeks, as there is no checklist that, when fulfilled, will ensure that you will get the opportunities that you are searching for. Develop your own style rather than trying to create something that you believe would eventually please someone.

The approach that you should utilize in the process of acquiring a music industry representative's attention regarding potential opportunities for career growth is crucial, and it is very important to make sure that the specifics of the situation and the nature of the specific goal are thoroughly understood. When it comes to achieving career growth, it is required to adopt the mentality of perfecting your craft, potential, and progress to a level where the opportunities will come to you, rather than the opposite, since this is the methodology to ensure sustainable progress. As with every other aspect of the music industry, the process of attracting interest from outside parties that can be beneficial for you is a matter of an ongoing, strategically formed procedure. It is a matter of business and your ability to add value to your name and showcase characteristics that the other parties will be interested in. Or, in other words, it is completely irrational to expect that a music industry participant would be intrigued by the opportunity to collaborate with you, if there is no particular aspect of your activity that can encourage such a choice. If you cannot provide any sort of potential for mutual benefit, there is no incentive for a professional party to work with you. Companies do not work with creators because they like their music, but because such relationships offer them progress and something that they need and do not have already. It is naïve to think that someone would offer you opportunities for growth and work with you for altruistic reasons. Hence, if you want to be in a position to stockpile assets that you can use in the process of generating quality interest, you have to perfect every aspect of your professional performance. Once this is achieved, offers will come to you. You need to be in a position to showcase your potential to attract people through numbers. Remember that your accomplishments are irrelevant if they cannot be explained and described with analytical figures. You should always make sure that the results of your work are quantifiable and comparable. Numbers showcase behavior; behavior shows the potential for a business to grow through utilizing the said behavior. Add value to your accomplishments. Do not just present your recent releases and shows. Showcase and explain how many sales you are generating with your products and what the amount of the audiences attending your concerts is. Convert your accomplishments and activities into numbers. Showcase every interaction as a potential profit.

You have to make sure that you are reaching the limit of your productivity and efficiency before bringing your profile to the attention of people that you want to work with. Do not get discouraged if you see some of your competitors establishing partnerships with certain companies either. Not every company (quite the opposite, actually) is in a position to offer you the career prospects that you need, so you should not be interested in partnering with such names. Smaller, inexperienced, or questionable establishments cannot provide you with opportunities for achieving a higher level of progress. They cannot provide you with sustainable results, and hence you need to concentrate on attracting true professionals, and the respective procedure requires a significant amount of time, preparation, and dedication. An act should very carefully and pragmatically consider and understand the fact that they should participate only in collaborations that they can actually can benefit from. Being a part of cooperation does not mean that the eventual advantageous results out of it would be spread equally to all of the participants. Hence, you have to ensure involvement in projects alongside other people that can certainly improve the state of your career, where the investments made in terms of time and effort would be properly returned and equally distributed.

The Culture of the Community

Do not go behind anyone's back, and do not count or rely on practices outside your professional field to achieve the desired results. Creating drama would never help you. The music sphere is not just an industry, it is a community. The most important and well-established participants in it are aware that you might have competitors, but you do not have enemies, as, at the end of the day, every artist, every professional, is part of the entertainment business cycle and its respective culture and you all need one another in order to progress and establish a fruitful career collectively. If one artist is successful and generates attention and interest to their activity, the whole industry benefits from it, and, consequentially, this provides chances for growth to every participant operating in this field, so it is incredibly pivotal to be aware of this concept and thoroughly understand the dynamics of the business before getting yourself involved in it. Every member of this field that would like to use the music community's platform to their benefit should commit to its requirements and comply with the unwritten code for respect and understanding, because if they do not do that, they will no longer have the privilege to partake in this field. Integrity is a decisive term in this sphere. Your reputation is as essential as the theoretical features of your brand and work, and sometimes even more than that. And considering the specific close operational mechanism of this field of work, you can be sure that if you showcase qualities and tendencies that do not correspond with the profile and the qualities of a music industry professional, your career status will be forever marked, and your brand will always be associated with opinions and statuses that will prevent you from your desired success, as you will burn a lot of bridges that you will need to cross at some point in order to reach your goals. Encourage and maintain relationships. Nurture and support your community. Be accessible and available at any point. With the successful and fruitful progress of your career, the levels of attention that regular people, fans, and professionals would surround you with would exponentially grow and increase. The effect of your actions would provoke will be progressively ascending. If you are able to create a nice impression, people will develop a long-lasting positive idea of you that will be naturally assigned to and associated with your brand and every respective activity that you might get yourself involved in. You will generate the biggest amount of praise, support and glorification for the tiniest positive gesture that you do. However, the same principle would be applicable to every negative move and every mistake that you allow yourself. If you afford yourself to not defend and represent the values that your profile and personality should be attached to, this would create and launch waves of disappointment and critique from the end consumer and the music community in general that, depending on the scale of the situation, can single-handedly erase years of hard work and progress and momentarily terminate your career.

CHAPTER 2

Mentality before Opportunity

The man with the average mentality, but with control, with a definite goal, and a clear conception of how it can be gained, and above all, with the power of application and labor, wins in the end.

—William Howard Taft

Considering the complexity of the current configuration of the music world and the variety of different and constantly changing standards and roles that artists of every status should perform and adjust to in order to ensure steady amount of progress to their respective brands, it is crucial for every act to perceive the notion of channeling and developing different mental states to the separate stages of their respective endeavors, as it is a common and perfectly reasonable misconception for young and fresh formations, especially, to be unable to correctly distinguish the different nature of their actions and appropriately recognize the specifics of the certain states of their lives. Hence, it is preferable and advisable for the following mental states to be differentiated and developed over the course of the establishment of a professional career:

- Personal mentality—personal attitude and character. The way you communicate and present yourself as a person
- Professional mentality—the way you handle all of the operations related to your work and act
- Artistic mentality—the way you approach your craft and activity as an artist

Ideally, the aforementioned three types of mentality should be fundamentally different in their essence, but they should also form the main character and features of your overall appearance in one logically and naturally constructed and homogeneous manner.

Personal Mentality

Commitment, Self-Reflection, and Resilience

The first step of undertaking and pursuing a career in the music industry is determining the level of your personal commitment (Do you think you have the commitment or you are certain that you possess it?) to the process of doing so and your realistic chances to achieve your goals in the most honest, realistic, and rational manner possible, as the decisive and fundamental component that the self-appraisal and professional evaluation are based on is the ability of being truthful with yourself in terms of your respective qualities and potential. There is no benefit in trying to assess yourself as someone or something that you are not. By doing so, you will only damage your chances to establish a fruitful and successful artist development process for your brand. The more information you have for yourself as a person and artist, the more beneficial and useful decision you will be able to determine. Hence, you will have to honestly and fairly evaluate the aspects and characteristics of your profile in order to be in a position to establish a promising and well-performing starting platform for your career development and, most importantly, concentrate on whether you possess the talent, the devotion, the belief in yourself and your specific gifts, and the drive to succeed with your eventual projects. The day that you stop believing in yourself, your capabilities, and your chances to succeed in your desired endeavors is the day that you fail. You should be pursuing your goals not because you want and you hope that you will achieve them at some point, but because you know you will, eventually. There is no place for second thoughts, hesitation, and uncertainty—strong and unwavering will is the first prerequisite that you can base your efforts on in order to generate a positive outcome. Discouragement is allowed only if you are in a position to overcome it. You cannot afford to worry about whether you made the right decision when approaching a career in music. You cannot afford to hesitate if your efforts are justified or not. You should avoid any overthinking and just keep pushing and working hard and progress toward your goals, regardless of the circumstances around you. Mental strength is the aspect and key indicator that separates failure from success for a music formation. Resilience in terms of mentality is the quality that should be constantly developed and emphasized on since this is the aspect that can transform the artist's fears and concerns to a sustainable drive. By controlling your perceptions, you are in a position to convert your challenges to opportunities and ensure that you can take advantage of every single situation that you are being presented to, despite of its character.

Nevertheless, you should also always be conscious of the fact that you are not tied to what your perspective of yourself is. Abandon the things that make you a person that you do not want to be or is not capable of achieving the results that you want. You can adjust, re-form, and evolve, but you will have to want it, not just experience the need to do it and undertake the whole process of improving yourself due to the feelings of obligation. Adapt to requirements, evolve your personal and professional qualities, and become the figure you know you have to be in order to reach the outcomes that you desire. This all starts with establishing the mentality of a winner, not only in your professional career, but in your personal life as well. You should not be satisfied with getting what you can. You should be aiming to get what you want, which essentially should be the concept behind your idea to establish a successful career in the music industry as well. If you want to achieve and do something, do not be scared to do so. Developing yourself as a professional does not mean that you should change your essence, preferences, appearance, and talents as a person and as an artist. It is not about transforming into something that you are not. It is about acknowledging the specifics of your profile and your strengths and weaknesses, and perfecting them so you can achieve the best possible version of yourself. Working on yourself surpasses the need of improving your professional qualities only and focusing on the aspects related to your career, necessarily. Understand that there is a noticeable difference between transforming, improving, and developing your natural and preexisting talents and qualities to the highest possible level and seeking evolution and cultivating a brand new set of skills that have not been connected with you before. These are two entirely different and contrasting in essence processes that should be allocated with an equally distributed amount of attention and effort, as every artist and professional should work hard toward achieving great results in both of these areas in order to ensure a high probability for success. In order to achieve personal development and explore the opportunities to become not just a better version of yourself, but a more equipped, skilled, and completed character and professional, you should not be afraid of understanding the concept of not staying in your lane and constantly proving to yourself that you can be a personality that you have not even imagined you can be by making decisions and undertaking actions that are not associated with your profile at all. Humans are creatures of behavior, and as such, a very small percentage of us tend to avoid pursuing activities outside our comfort zone, unless absolutely necessary. Do not be afraid to do things that are shocking to you and test the limits of your comfort. Aim to look at and enjoy opportunities that can help you to reinvent yourself. The indication that this process is being successful is when the feeling of being uncomfortable in your actions and with your decisions occurs, as this is a clear sign that you are moving in the right direction of exceeding your predetermined perceptions of yourself. When reaching this level of self-awareness, the only thing that you should do is to continue forward and push even further with the idea of continuing your transformation by increasing and encouraging your participation in choices and moves that would develop you to the person that you are aiming to be.

Responsibility

Always point the thumb and not the finger. The first instinct of a musician when facing a failure should be acknowledging the significance of their own actions and decisions and concentrating on finding their own fault for the unfortunate results. Think about what you did wrong, analyze, and assess what you could do better in order to prevent the negative outcome, even if it is clear that the main problem was caused by circumstances out of your control. Since, regardless of whether an unfortunate turn of events occurred due to your fault or due to reasons out of your control, it is always the artist's responsibility and you should accept that. Even if outside factors are the cause of the problem, it is still your fault that you have not predicted or took them properly in consideration when planning your respective actions. The worst possible tendency that an artist can adopt is placing blame on external factors and people, once certain results are not successful and positive as expected and desired. Being part of a fruitful and well-performing music act requires extreme ownership as a leader and being capable of adopting the role of the main figure of your brand; hence you should be capable of taking full liability for your actions when needed. Passionately seek advice and input, but make your own decisions. And, ultimately, always go with your gut. Inner dialogue matters. In a variety of different situations, your conscious would be the main corrective that you can trust and rely on in terms of your decisions. Hence, it is of critical importance to make sure that your inner self is the most rational interlocutor that you can listen to. Weigh the advice you are given by people that you trust, but at the end of the day listen to your instincts, because whether certain move turns out to be the right or the wrong answer, you have to be able to blame yourself and no other people for your eventual failures. There is no place for excuses. Do not blame anything or anyone, but yourself for your eventual failures. It is never the wrong decision if you do the right thing, regardless of what the consequences might be. Remember that there is not anything that you should regret if you have taken the most rational and logical option at the time that is also suitable to your personality and personal specifications, even if it leads to an abrupt negative outcome. It is doubtlessly pivotal to always ensure utilizing the most appropriate, right option and not letting anything else disturb your stance on the matter.

Time Management

Do not waste your time and take advantage of it, because the way you take advantage of your time is the marker that can separate you from your competitors. Every second gives you the opportunity to do something that your career can benefit from. Every second that you do not use in this manner is a missed chance for growth that another artist is taking advantage of in order to become better than you, while you are not utilizing your chances for progress. Wasting time is an activity that you cannot afford to practice, especially if you really want to truly succeed in this industry.

Professional Mentality

Perspicaciousness

Considering the incredibly difficult and complicated path that the artists should dedicate all of their time, effort, talents, passion, and devotion to in order to succeed in their respective desired endeavors, any potential hard-to-overcome obstacles and setbacks could be very demoralizing and damaging in terms of mindset and mental health. Therefore, it is essential for every participant in the music industry cycle to understand and closely follow the principle of not taking any negative or disappointing outcomes, which do not meet pre-stated expectations in an emotional and personal manner. The lack of ability to objectively and rationally approach certain tasks related to your professional duties is a big obstacle that is being presented by the different parties in the industry in terms of the separate aspects of a professional activity. Many professionals tend to trust their emotional opinions and follow their instincts when it comes to approaching certain projects, which always makes it very difficult to achieve results that are reasonable and well deserved. Usually, a

considerable amount of performers lack the ability to honestly and correctly judge themselves and the situations that they experience, which
lead to very damaging (for them) consequences in terms of their career
progress—developing lack of respect and false evaluation of their talents
and the potential of their ideas, establishing inaccurate sense of entitle-
ment, arrogance, and so on, as all of these things are prerequisites for
constructing a mindset that can massively decrease any chances for a good
career in music. Some acts stop investing work and effort in their career,
yet they have high expectations regarding the results that they receive and
tend to blame everyone but themselves if the said results do not match
their assumptions and notions. Actions beget results. It sounds very logical and understandable; however, lots of musicians tend to overlook and
perceive this concept subconsciously. If you want results, you need to
attract them. You have to earn your blessing, because it will not come to
you if you do not encourage it to do so. Lots of artists expect help and demand results without being able to contribute to their own success. There
are no successful artists that have received the chance to be prosperous,
famous, and well known as an option. They all have received it as a result
of their approach. Always consider that it is not the industry's fault if
you are not generating the outcomes you want. Certain groups of people
always seek help and are very vocal about not receiving it in the process
of their career development, but at the same time constructive criticism
is always claimed as unreasonable by them. Overall, many artists would
present themselves as developed professionals and have high demands
toward their products and craft; however, they would still tend to base
important decisions regarding their growth on personal and emotional
perceptions and preferences that are not related with the professional aspect of their activity in any way and, at the same time, would refuse to
acknowledge the need of evaluating their own role and importance in the
process of achieving the results that they desire. Have you noticed who are
the musicians and the professionals that constantly emphasize on the fact
that they have so much to learn and they are only grasping the potential
of their respective talents and potential? The most successful ones. Having
said that, you should be aware that you are probably not as good as you
think you are as well. The first indication for insufficient knowledge and
experience and the need for significant improvement of your awareness

is the idea that you possess all the knowledge, training, and capabilities that you might possibly need in order to establish a successful career. The nature of the music business is such that the longer amount of time you spend operating in it and the more goals you achieve, the more you would start realizing that the less you know about your professional activity.

Requirements for Efficiency within a Competitive Field

An act should acknowledge and always respect the notion that the only object for observation should be their own career and development. The most prominent mistake made by a variety of artists around the globe is concentrating on other formations' progress and careers. You have your own timeline and you should not let progress achieved by your competitors to distract your attention from the only aspect of your activity that deserves all of your energy and attention—your personal craft. Perfect yourself. Expand the potential of your qualities and do not compare yourself to anyone. You are your own cycle and as such you have to understand that, ultimately, outside factors that are not related to your particular case are not in a position to diminish the successful rate of your work, and hence, it is only an irrational waste of energy and time to concentrate your awareness on that. Never let your motivation and desire to work and succeed with your talents be affected by the progress achieved by your rivals. It is very easy for an artist to lose a significant amount of drive and wish for growth when they see someone else achieving the results that they are struggling to generate. It is very frustrating to ob serve success while you are doing everything in your power and beyond to achieve it, and a mental environment of this sort can most certainly very negatively affect not only the development of your own career, but also your personal well-being, especially if you are doubtlessly devoted to reaching your goals. Experiencing feelings of envy and jealousy toward the developments and achievements of your competitors is a clear indication that you are in a critical need of further improving, enhancing, and exceeding your talents, product, work ethic, and personal investments in your career and that you are most certainly not on the right path to success. Basing your perceptions on other artists' activities or on the status of your ego is a clear sign that you feel fear regarding the possibility of them being better than you, which leads to feelings of self-belittlement and self-awareness, and such turn of events occurs only when you see logical and reasonable evidence to support your conclusions. If you are truly successful and better than your competitors, you will naturally and genuinely not only avoid spending unnecessary energy in the process of following and emotionally involving yourself in their respective endeavors, but you will be actually willing to support their success, because if you are and if you know that you are the best in what you do, you will be subconsciously comfortable and at peace that no one can beat you at your own game. Take confidence in your strengths; do not take confidence from other people's weaknesses. There is not a more clear indication for the dysfunction of your professional mentality if you rely on your competitors' failures to feel positive and optimistic about your own career, as such a mindset is possessed only by people who clearly do not have the needed qualities and self-belief to undertake the right approach and concentrate all of their efforts and energy on developing themselves, rather than wasting their focus and concentration on people and activities that are, in no way, related to the progress of their career. Remember, if you feel the need of receiving justification that you are doing better than your competitors, you are probably not better than them at all.

Financial Considerations

Quality is not compatible with cost-efficiency. Improving and developing your profile is a process that is not suitable to trying to be economical in terms of your financial investments during the beginning stage of your career. Money very often comes very late than expected, so you should carry about money only so you can provide yourself with enough options for growth. Do not perceive the revenue that you are generating with your professional activity as profit. Consider it as funds that you can invest in operations, which can help you to improve the product that you are offering further—better equipment, bigger budget for production, promotional activities, advertisement, and so on. You should not be necessarily interested in money as a resource to raise the level of your personal status, but to improve your professional one instead. Allocating funds to your career and activity is not a cost; it is an investment. Act smart with your earnings. Do not be careless, but avoid being overprotective with them as well. Invest to receive.

Artistic Mentality

The Artist–Product Interrelationship

You should try to be cognitive and recognize the inherent development that your product is experiencing through your achieved maturity as a musician and as a person at any point in time. Your art directly represents the state and the specifics of your personality. The music that a person creates is the perfect embodiment of their personal and unique traits and characteristics; it is the most honest, genuine, and authentic collection of emotions, showcasing every distinctive quality developed through life. Having said that, an artist should be aware of the fact that they cannot expect or aim to develop their craft if they are not ready or capable of developing themselves as people first. If you want to change your music, change yourself, change your life, interact with new people, and broaden your horizons from every different perspective of your existence. You will be never able to prepare different concoctions with the same ingredients, so if you want to constantly provide your audience with consistently original, unique, and memorable content that has the potential to establish an authentic emotional connection with the general audience, make sure that you are being subjected to different influences as well and that you are always in a position to expand and advance your own personality. Develop yourself to develop your craft. Creative people always have to keep creating, and you always have to almost reinvent yourself and what you are doing, without worrying about other people's opinions. Considering the strong entrepreneurial approach and nature that every aspect of an artist's career is based on, the significance of the trial-and-error methodology for the process of professional and personal growth is undeniable. The more time, effort, and practice you invest in your respective endeavors, the better you will become. Do not stop writing songs, practicing your presence, or communicating with people, because you will learn and acknowledge new information that can help you to perfect your qualities each time that you do so. It is a common situation for artists to find themselves in a position where they are frustrated due to not seeing achieved progress in their craft, but at the same time, they cannot find the motivation to work on expanding their skills, which creates one very negative and damaging cycle of thoughts and mentality, preventing a brand to grow. Hence, it is crucial for an act to always be open to find new influences, inspirations, motives, and goals to follow, as it is impossible for any creative individual to expect different results while doing and utilizing the same approach, methodology, and activities over and over again. Do not respect the status quo—the only people that can achieve sustainable success are the ones that can envision what their product could be, rather than what it actually is. The artists changing the world and the landscape around them are the ones that want to achieve this effect. You will never be able to have significant influence on your audience if this is not something that you genuinely want to achieve.

Strive for Excellence

Developing the killer instinct mentality is an aspect of the performing artist's activity that should never be neglected and should be, actually, prioritized. An artist should always strive to represent qualities that they would like the audience to associate them with, even subconsciously. In the current oversaturated market, where thousands of acts are aiming to achieve one goal, which only a few names would be in a position to, essentially, such as generating sustainable success, it is of significant importance to showcase an exceptional level of talent, charisma, and dedication to your craft. You cannot expect people to perceive you as an incredible performer and unquestionably support you if you do not show that their opinions are reasonable. Whether we are talking about creating a song, releasing a video, or performing a show, you should always make sure to be in a position to showcase how much better and more attractive your brand is to everyone than the one of your competitors. It is about this competitive nature to beat yourself. Create a song that is better than your previous one. Be a better player and a more complete professional than you were yesterday. Beat the performance that you just had on stage. It will take time to get competitive. It is absolutely fundamental to be aggressive and experience the natural and genuine urge to compete with others and showcase your value in an intense environment in order to prove the characteristics that not many people possess, but are, however, essential aspects of the mentality, which a music industry participant should develop in order to build the most efficient and successful approach for delivering desired results in the music business. Completely changing your moral values and instincts and adjusting them to the specific needs of the aforementioned profile of a competitive personality is, of course, not an easily accessible procedure that can be most definitely completed properly, but it is, however, possible to modify the shape of your personality to a level that will enable you to at least utilize your unique characteristics in the process of forming an approach that can provide you with the general understanding of the method that you should implement toward the idea of presenting yourself as superior to your competitors, in terms of your qualities and value in the music industry.

CHAPTER 3

Develop Yourself before Developing Your Career

The drive to close the gap between near-perfect and perfect is the difference between great and unstoppable.

—Tim Grover

Implementation of Knowledge and Understanding to Your Activity

If you work and strive to achieve a certain result, you should be ready and prepared to undertake and embrace the process of reaching it. Do not initiate professional relationships that you are not ready to participate in and do not seek opportunities that you are not in a position to take full advantage of. Involving yourself in the process of completing a certain project, regardless of its nature, prematurely and without possessing the right vision and mentality to do so might not only fail to give the result you want or expect, but actually damage the overall state of your progress. Situations of this kind are simply bad and irrational investments, where you waste not only your potential, productivity, and energy but also other people's as well, as creating impression of an act with undeveloped and questionable attitude, understanding, and approach is most certainly not an opinion that you would like to assign to your brand, considering that such impressions are very hard to be modified once strongly established, regardless of how your career would eventually unfold. Be professional and ready for what you need to do. Regardless of what the exact situation is, an artist should acknowledge it and work toward perfecting their overall approach and activity in the respective field of the opportunities, which they would like to utilize. Experience and work ethic matter, so do not neglect them. You are more likely to receive the chance for growth if the party that is providing you with it is ensured and certain that you are capable, ready, and in a position to treat it with the required attitude, respect, and professionalism.

Learning and Self-Sufficiency

If you can learn something, you can do anything, because you understand the concept of utilizing your own skills and qualities in the process of adopting an unknown concept. Hence, one of the most beneficial principles that you should try to adopt with your career is the idea of being self-sufficient and being the best version of yourself. Be as independent as possible and in control of absolutely everything. Do not let external factors dictate your decisions and minimize the effect or the significance that other people have on your professional growth. The more you learn, the less you will be dependent on the work and the dedication of other people and the more you will be in the control of your career's progress. By learning different skills and perfecting your qualities, you are also adding ancillary value to your profile and you are providing further indications to the music industry that you are a responsible, professional, and dedicated individual who is not hesitant to participate in the procedure of developing and reinventing themselves, while pursuing career in music. You showcase adaptiveness and dedication to earn your success, rather than just receiving it. You have to be flexible with your work approach; you have to be open-minded, and if you do not know something, it is important to say and admit that you do not know it in order to learn about it. That is an essential matter of understanding, because the music business is not simple; there are not any rules that you can follow and can guarantee you specific results, unlike in other industries. Do not count on other people and do not wait for someone to help you, unless absolutely necessary. You have access to everything that you need in order to succeed, and it is only up to you to take advantage of all of the opportunities that are being available and open to you. Absorb and extract the right information related to your activities that you need in order to progress. Every piece of data and guidance that you might need in the process of developing your career is available to you and you do not need to be taught or told what and how to do a particular action in order to get the results that you are aiming for. There is no better way to acquire information than acquiring it yourself, whether through theoretical methods or personal experience.

Researching is pivotal, but only when it is performed correctly. Gathering information is essential to develop knowledge; however, information should not be perceived as guidance. Always consider the main goal of the process of gathering data of any sort—to collect the understanding you need in order to develop appropriate skills relevant to your career and professional goals, not encyclopedic knowledge. A vast majority of acts tend to follow and apply advice and instructions from different professionals during the early stages of their careers. While the interest to expand your personal understanding of different matters in the music industry and be willing to accept the expertise of other professionals and use their experience to your benefit can be proven very beneficial, it is important for an artist to realize that this is not, ultimately, a winning approach. The music industry community, the people you follow and admire, and your friends might be able to provide you with well-constructed, logical, and professional general thoughts related to the music industry and your particular career; however, chances are that utilizing their direct opinions and instructions would not give you the results that you are expecting, just because the fact that even a certain method that has provided positive results when applied to one case cannot in any way guarantee that would do the same when applied to another one, due to the strong connection that should be considered between an action and the specifics of a certain situation. The best advice is not coming from the most successful personality; it is coming from the most experienced and intelligent one, so do not always rely on words coming from well-known names as well. Yes, in the majority of the situations, these two different figures would overlap, but that is not always the case and you have to distinguish these different options.

Develop Your Professional Craft

Success is generated by profit, which is the product of interest, caused by quality and uniqueness. Regardless of the complexity of the mechanisms in the music industry, fundamentally there is one concept that will always dictate the evolution of this business and, consequently—, the motives of everyone involved in it—the fact that the ability to generate attention is the essential and ultimate core of the success in this field. The role of an entertainer is to entertain people. So, if you want to make a career undertaking such duties, learn what attracts and maintain people's attention.

The main priority of a person involved in the entertainment industry should not be to achieve a successful career as a final destination of the respective career path, but to reach the maximum potential and development as a person and a professional figure. Aim to improve yourself and raise your level of proficiency, experience, and talent and use this desire as guidance for your progress and not the simple idea of being successful. Perfection, excellence, and greatness are prerequisites for the establishment of a long-term, fruitful, and lucrative activity in the business, and in order to add these qualities to your arsenal, you should first concentrate on yourself and assess your strive to generate a successful career in the music field from the point of view where you are the strongest and most reliable tool that you can use in the process of gaining the respective accomplishments that you want. Working toward success, necessarily, is a decision that requires truly different mentality and understanding, which at the end of the day, can only change the focus of an artist to the idea of developing skills and profile, which are capable of advancing to short-term results, rather than having the characteristics to form an ongoing success rate. Applying diligence and discipline to your productivity as an artist is absolutely necessary. Do not lose sight of the fact that being good at what you do is important. The need for constant self-improvement is crucial. In the current stage of the oversaturated music market, there are thousands of artists who are aiming to achieve your goals that you are in a direct competition with. Chances are that they might be more talented than you, that they are in a position to invest more money and time in their career, and that they might be surrounded by better circumstances for development in general. Hence, it is necessary to completely dedicate your time, energy, and thoughts to the process of getting better at what you do and be better than your competitors in your respective field. Realize that there is always room for improvement. No matter how good, talented, or perfected you feel you are, you can always be better and you should always aim to improve yourself. You cannot be better than anyone if you are not the best version of yourself. You should always follow the concept that, regardless of how good you are, you are never as good as you should be. Be comfortable with yourself but also know that you can always achieve more and you always possess the potential to perfect your talents and improve your product further, regardless of how proud you might of with the current quality of the results that you are creating. Do not compete with others. Compete with yourself and make others compete with you.

The truth is that allocating a notable amount of attention to the beginning development phase of your activity as an artist and a content creator from the early stages of your career is a more efficient, fruitful, and necessary strategy, which can ensure a better flow and results with the time, as it gives you the opportunity to correctly shape and form the mentality and the general approach during the initial stages of the process of establishing the specifics of your craft, rather than working toward the very exhausting and time-consuming task to change and modify already constructed perceptions and notions that you might need to do if you do not attend this process with the needed regard during the right time, which is always a very challenging and, mostly, an inefficient process.

Creating Music

Complexity does not represent perfection. It is quite the opposite, as a matter of fact. Regardless of the aspect of your career that you might be involved in, you have to understand that developing your actions and ideas on the principle of perplexing your work and efforts is not a method that increases and improves the quality of the results that you are producing. In reality, only people who lack the knowledge, creativity, and the vision to present a genuinely unique concepts and ideas hide their inability to do so by unnecessarily complicating their work. An exceptional idea or content does not need to be presented in a sophisticated manner to impress or gain attention. Especially when it comes to the topic of establishing a successful profile in the music industry, which is a task that very much depends on your ability to affect the perceptions of as many people as possible, it is important for an artist to be capable of providing a naturally engaging, easily comprehensible, and accessible product that possess the characteristics to present its main idea as smoothly and instinctively to a large portion of the audience, regardless of the difference in perceptions, understandings, and personal specifics that these people might have in terms of digesting an end product. There is a huge difference between being a good musician and a good songwriter. The extent of your technical talent to perform does not mean that you have the ability to create good, memorable, and relatable music. The fact that you are a good instrumentalist, that you have significant theoretical knowledge, and that you are capable of playing multiple instruments does not mean that you offer a better product. Music is not a checklist.

Performing Music

The live performance show is an event that showcases the effect and the influence that music has on both the audience and the musician at their most purest, raw, and emotional form. It is all about the level of emotional connection that an act is capable of establishing with its audience. In order for a pure and genuine connection of this sort to be established, it is important for a performer to be honest and devoted to its true intentions. There are many aspects relevant to an artist's career that can be deliberately developed in a certain way or manner, but when it comes to a live performance, the artist should be ready and possess the ability to truly expose their genuine identity to the crowd in order to instill a specific atmosphere, which would help accentuate the unique experience that the artist can provide to their audience. Controlling smaller crowds and guiding their actions in the process of establishing a high level of entertainment throughout a live performance is always a way more difficult and complicated task, in comparison to providing a large audience with the experience that they would be impressed by, especially considering the undeveloped and rather unpolished approach that fresh acts might have during their early shows. For example, when performing live, the artist must understand that a flawless technical prowess is not the aspect that should be emphasized on, and it can never substitute the effect that the human interaction process can achieve. Body language matters more than anything else. You should always ensure that you are encouraging mutual understanding and comfort through your actions, and in order to do that, you should be ready and able to readjust your mental approach toward performing a show. It is important to not approach an event as an opportunity for professional benefit, but as a chance to expose and showcase your personality and the value of your talent to the people supporting you and enjoy the whole experience while doing so. You should not aim to act, look, and be perceived in a certain manner that is not related to your personal characteristics, but to find the ultimate configuration of live presence that can connect the audience with the purest form of your essence as an artist.

Develop Your Working Environment

The significance of establishing strong, positive, and fruitful working environment based on trust, mutual understanding, and respect is undeniable. The selection of people and characters that you choose to surround yourself with while undertaking a career in the music industry is of incredibly crucial importance for the establishment of a successful and well-operating activity. The effect and influence that a certain character's presence can place on your evolution as a professional—whether in a direct or a subconscious manner—is most definitely a strong factor that an artist should be aware of. A lot of motivations and drive for success is coming from the people that you are cooperating with. At the same time, internal conflicts will damage your music, so stellar working environment is more important than what most people's perceptions indicate. Especially when it comes to the communication forming the path of a career progress, it is an undeniable necessity to be in touch with personalities that endorse your advancement to the person that you need to become in order to achieve your goals and encourage your evolution from both personal and professional points of view, rather than attaching yourself to people who cannot provide you with the ambition and drive to surpass your current situation, position, and status. Be in contact with people who would help you to become the person you want to be, not the ones who would encourage you to stay and be comfortable with your current profile. When the correct time for forming your team and choosing people to work with comes, always go with the person who is the most excited and in love with your talent and believes in it. It may not necessarily be the biggest name or one who has the greater experience, the most money, or the most success, but a person who is doubtlessly passionate about you and as passionate as you are about your craft, because only such people would be genuinely invested in your project and would put the amount of effort and dedication in your career that you deserve and require in order to achieve your goals.

Every problem that can be a potential big obstacle for building a healthy relationship (which is something essential and needed in order for everyone involved in the cycle of professional activities to benefit from them) should be acknowledged early. It is crucial to be able to genuinely and naturally collaborate with a party involved in the progress of your career, and sometimes experiencing problems with this can be easily sensed by every side and lead to very damaging, tense, and toxic atmosphere. And there is not a party to be blamed if the results in this direction are not positive; sometimes the perceptions in terms of working approach are different and not compatible with each other, and it is indisputably irrational for everyone to waste time and effort in a cooperation that just does not have a positive working environment, which neither of the participants in the respective partnership is happy with.

Leadership

Leadership is important. Maslow in his hierarchy of needs states factors such as safety of the environment they operate in, sense of belonging in the team, self-esteem, and perhaps an opportunity to seek self-actualization as some of the aspects that the leader figure should be concentrating on when it comes to establishing a connection in a team-oriented environment. There is no success without team. Whether you are a solo artist or a formation, your team is your unit. There is no time for ego when it comes to establishing the dynamics of your inner activity, in which the utilization of the authoritative approach is imperative. Being part of a professional music entity is an incredibly challenging, difficult, and unexpectedly complicated process from a moral point of view as well, as you will need to often base decision on an approach that can guarantee you the results that you need, not the ones that you necessarily want. You should always remember that democratically made decisions within the support cast of a music act form the fair and honest method to navigate the direction of your career. However, these decisions are often based on personal compromises and finding a solution that multiple people would feel comfortable with, rather than finding the best decision that would be most beneficial in the particular situation. Sometimes an authoritative approach is needed, because in multiple cases there will be an individual that understands the characteristics of the specific situation better than anyone else, and regardless of what your position and role within the career of the artist is, you should be capable of acknowledging the potential of a person to determine the correct actions in a particular situation and recognize once an idea is better and more logical than yours, in general, for example. Assign roles, request results, and encourage effort. Whether you are a solo artist with a team of managers, agents, and press representatives or an independent band with members that are taking care of everything related to your professional activity, it is necessary to ensure that all of the participants forming your project are acting as one unit and are a part of one homogeneous and cohesive process, where every single party is aware of the targeted goal and it is in a position to approach all of this with a mindset and mentality familiar to the other members of the operation.

Separate business from friendship and never conflate these two terms. Friendships are not business relationships; hence, it is important to clearly recognize and distinguish one from the other, or else you might find yourself in an extremely tensed and damaging situations, where you will see yourself in circumstances not only where the positive progress of your work is being threatened, but where your personal life could be affected as well. Incorporating personal connections and relationships in your work can be a very attractive concept at first sight, but it most definitely contains more risks than opportunities for success. Involving personal matters in your career means that you will have to often consider your personal position in the process of making decisions regarding your career and compromise your analytical thinking and strategy. The professional development of your act is not a place for you to base your decisions on personal preferences. Do not work with friends, work and cooperate with colleagues, and establish connections where you will not have to tolerate mediocrity and compromise your brand because of personal connections and feelings. Strive for excellence is needed in every single endeavor that is relevant to your career, so you cannot afford any emotional attachments toward people related to your activity, who are capable to affect and influence the quality of your productivity in a negative manner.

Dealing with Negativity

One of the most important qualities that an artist should master and be able to actively use on a constant basis during a career in music is dealing and handling the negativity that a profile in the entertainment industry will be undeniably exposed to. After all, one of the main goals of an artist is to establish as wider public reach as possible, exposing their products to as many people as possible. In order to achieve that, a profile in the music business has to be incredibly available and accessible, and sometimes, completely naturally, this will not be generating positive results, because your profile will not be exposed only to people with the potential to appreciate and enjoy your product, but to those who are going to dislike it as well. The risks of the promotional process to generate negative responses and feedback are significantly lower when it comes to businesses that want and aim to develop locally, but when you are a participant in the entertainment industry and your mission is to achieve global exposure and interest, you have to be prepared and anticipate the highest degree of negative backslash, especially considering the gargantuan capacity of the Internet and the modern technologies to amplify the effects of your marketing and their ability to reach plenty of different audiences and target groups, which might not be necessarily interested in what you can offer at all. Remember that general response and feedback to your activities do not define you as an artist, but define your professional approach. Negative opinions do not necessarily indicate that you are not talented or that your product is bad, but that you are maybe not approaching your craft in the best possible way. Rebuke on your work is actually a great indication for achieved exposure and influence—not the opposite. Receiving such is actually, in fact, the only sign that the reach of your music is expanding to new audiences and territories. Only once that your music is heard by people that are not interested in your career, who also decide to spend time and effort to comment on it or think about it, you can confirm that the activity of your work is progressing in the right direction. It is not possible for a successful act to generate only positive reactions. Formations that receive only encouragements and appraisal are such that have very limited reach for their music, where their activities are assessed only by personal friends and family and a closed circle of people, in general. Such comments and responses should not be perceived by the artist as a realistic, rational feedback, since such opinions are clearly not based on genuine and natural reference to the music aspect of the artist's activity, but on an emotional reasoning, which does not have any relation to the actual valuable characteristics of the respective career.

Professional Influence

An artist should understand and properly recognize the limit of their activities and their respective reach in terms of influence within the music industry. An act should be culpable and held accountable to being capable to present its brand, talent, and professionalism to the highest possible standards in order to ensure generating the most beneficial results out of certain chances; however, one thing should be properly noted—you cannot control how people would perceive you, your music, or your career.

There is a limit to what you can do to progress your professional growth to the next level, and it is extremely damaging to start blaming yourself if the results that you are receiving are not the desired ones due to reasons out of your control. At the end of the day, music is a subjective matter, and as such, there will be many professionals that would not provide you with any chances for career progress due to not seeing the potential for mutual development, due to not believing that you have what it takes to be successful, or simply because they do not enjoy what you are doing and how you are doing it. And that is completely fine. But you should never take such situations personally and you should never let yourself start forming certain personal negative feelings, anger, animosity, or resentment toward music professionals who do not perceive you as you would like them to. The fact that they are not giving you the chances that you have expected from them is not because they have anything against you on a personal level, but just because they do not see any opportunity for professional benefit that they can take advantage of at this particular stage of your career. You should also remember that, at the end of the day, it is business, not personal. Throughout your career, you will probably need to experience being denied or dismissed in terms of certain opportunities multiple times. Rejections do not define you, so holding grudges is not an activity that would bring any positives to your profile. Avoid dealing with such situations with a personal attitude, it is just business. It is all about the mutual benefit, and once the party, which you want or need to collaborate with, sees the potential for such, you will receive your chance for development.

General Negativity

The easy, common, and most rational way to handle the negative influence that antipathetic comments and opinions might have on your activity is to completely ignore and dismiss them. However, a music industry professional should also always acknowledge and appreciate that every event or opportunity in their career—regardless of its nature and whether it is good or bad—presents a chance for development and benefit. If people feel a certain way about you or if there is a well-spread, shared, and established perception of you, there is probably a valid reason for that and you need to acknowledge and, eventually, work on it too. Do not avoid or be negligent or defensive toward impressions and opinions—they are the corrective that you need to consider in order to assess your activity objectively and, to a large extent, the information that can help you improve your general methods in terms of approach and appearance. Aim to gather different opinions and points of view. Different perspectives lead to new possibilities, opportunities, and ways for improvement. By understanding and gathering knowledge about the way that your music is being perceived by different people, you will be able to look at your craft and the specifics of your actions from different angles, as this can help you to understand your product and talents better, in more of an in-depth manner, and give you the idea of how you can improve, adjust, or perfect your abilities and qualities in the process of developing your unique style and presence through your product. Every negative occurrence is providing you with the chance to showcase your value and express the qualities that you would like your audience to be aware of and, essentially, turn negativity into positives. Although this might be a great struggle for personalities that are not naturally equipped to deal with such situations in this manner, you should always aim to expose your high morals, style, and class and be the bigger person in that particular case. Hence, you should make sure that events and situations of this kind are anticipated and expected, since once you are mentally prepared for them, you will know how to treat and handle them in the most beneficial and effective for your career way. The utilization of your intelligence instead of your emotions when it comes to experiencing and handling issues of this nature is a certain necessity. You should be aware that you are always becoming the losing side in an argument even by just participating in the process of communicating and interacting with people who are irradiating you with pointless and negative attitude. Aiming to prove yourself and trying to explain your moves to someone who does not care about you or your product is absolutely useless and a pure waste of time and energy. You are not generating anything beneficial for yourself or your career, but you are actually only fulfilling the purpose of the people who are initiating all of this—giving them attention and bothering yourself. You should be concentrating only on sharing your art and its essence to the world and expanding your audience while doing so. Everything else can be classified as a counterproductive activity. Do not burn bridges by giving a platform to your emotions and kill the rude, unproductive, and harmful comments that you might receive with kindness. Always take the higher road, even if you are being an object of huge disrespect. You got to respect everybody. There is absolutely nothing beneficial for your career that you can achieve by being aggressive, defensive, or emotional. If you create something that you believe in, if your craft is something that you truly stand behind, then no matter what anybody says about it or thinks about it, it will always be worth it to you. You should be making music for yourself and just hope that it affects other people in the way you want. You have to continue pursuing this thing you love no matter how much it feels that you are swimming against the current. Every successful artist will have to go through such a process multiple times through their respective professional life, so you should anticipate and embrace yourself for this process as well.

CHAPTER 4

The Bigger Picture Is the Only One You Have to Focus on

He who sacrifices his conscience to ambition burns a picture to obtain the ashes.

—Chinese Proverb

Understanding Success

The fine line between failure and success in every endeavor, but specifically in the music industry, is marked by persistence and the ability to constantly maintain high levels of drive and ambition to achieve your most desired results. Regardless of how difficult and overwhelming the obstacles you might need to overcome or the position that you might find yourself in may be, you will undoubtedly find yourself victorious in the end of such cycles if you ensure full dedication to your efforts and persistence with your actions. Success will unfold, eventually. It is undeniable. Your career performance and the overall level of success that you can achieve are mostly a matter of self-belief and confidence, rather than actual ability and qualities—the most successful participants in this industry are never necessarily the most talented, but the most persistent, devoted, and hardworking ones. Trusting yourself, your talents, and your potential determines the direction of your development and growth, as the specifics of your self-awareness control your actions in terms of the goals and the ideas you have toward your professional activity and the way that you approach and deal with the respective obstacles, which you have to overcome in order to prove yourself successful. Believing in yourself is a notion that dictates your efforts in the process of shaping yourself to the person who is able to achieve the results, which you are aiming to accomplish. Most people are not successful because they do not possess the desire to be, subconsciously. Every person possesses the chance to achieve and reach their desires, but due to already established prejudices and perceptions, they decide not to do so. It is you against the world and you better be ready to place your bets on yourself in this battle, if you want to win it in the end.

Success is not measured by the amount of money you earn or the achieved levels of influence, fame, or attention that you generate. Success is a term that implies and describes your ability to have the freedom to live your life the way you want to. So, it is important to clearly define what the meaning behind this word for you is, personally, in order to make sure that you are undertaking the right steps in the process of following the right goals. Personal success and professional success are two different terms that should not be mixed in their essence by the artist. However, once the final destinations of these two channels match, the artist can be assured and certain that this is an indication and a sign that their mind is on the right path to success in the music business. You are not working toward a profession and a career in the conventional sense of the word. You are working toward achieving your calling, so you have to almost accept the pursuance of your goals as an obsession. For a long period of time—especially if you want to reach the highest possible levels of this business—your activity as an artist should not be the first thing on your mind; it should be the only thing on it, no exceptions. The road to achieving your goals will be hard and your personal life will suffer to a larger extent than you can even imagine, but you should be ready to pay this price and to be actually willing to do it as well. Possessing this strong desire and drive for greatness and success, in most cases, is a quality that is either present or absent in a person's character and is almost impossible to be taught in reality. However, from a psychological point of view, the nature of a person's essence is such that it always aspires to reach certain achievements marked as essential for the given personality. Hence, even if the artist's personality features do not include ardent passion for prosperity, they should make sure that they are capable of maximizing their present potential for drive and ambition and to take advantage of it while seeking career affluence.

What does sustainable career mean? Ultimately, this is a term that represents the artist's ability to be in a position where they can earn enough money to satisfy their living needs and be comfortable and able to concentrate their full attention and working potential on the process of improving their respective craftsmanship. In order for this level of activity to be achieved, you have to ensure a high level of monetization to your respective professional projects. Or, in other words, if you want to be able to do what you do, you have to make sure that you are earning money. You can utilize and invest your full potential, capacity, personal qualities, and talents in your career only once your mind does not have to worry about other aspects of your life. Hence, it is important to make sure that all of your basic needs are always met and that your mind is not overwhelmed by any thoughts that might harm your full dedication to your craft in order to fortify the productivity and quality of your working potential, which you need to utilize in order to eventually gain the accomplishments that you are seeking.

Career Path

Start by taking advantage of every opportunity for growth, even for free. It is of significance to be able and ready to take advantage of any eventual chances for growth that you might be presented with, especially during the very early stages of your professional evolution. Achieving conventional success in the industry is an operation, which very much depends on external factors that the artists very often cannot affect with their actions, and most of the times, chances for immediate, desired, and crucial growth come suddenly and unexpected, when they cannot be anticipated. Therefore, the artist must acknowledge and be aware of the fact that appropriate opportunities for career progress are not to be missed and they should always be taken advantage of. Most of the people tend to let their personal fears affect their rational decision in such circumstances and choose personal comfort over the possibility of professional growth, which is an approach that completely and massively reduces your chances to succeed. Promptness, swiftness, and preparedness are core qualities for every participant in the entertainment business, but it is also highly likely that during the course of your career, you will find yourself in a situation where you will have to act immediately, in a rapid, yet strict, manner in order to take advantage of a career-defining opportunity. As a matter of fact, you will most probably encounter the chances that you have been putting an incredible amount of time and effort to generate and that can elevate your career instantly as an abrupt occurrence. Having said that, it is necessary for an artist to anticipate such turn of events and be prepared to think and act quickly, expeditiously, and hastily in order to be able to benefit from every single possibility for growth that might become available in due course. It is likely that you will be asked to fill a suddenly freed support slot for a big concert, to perform on radio or accept a touring offer in a matter of minutes, so the quality of being not only constantly ready to eventually commit to this sort of opportunities, but also capable of organizing yourself and work under tight and strict deadlines, without letting such circumstances damage the value of your product (regardless of its nature), is most certainly an asset that can put you ahead of your competition in numerous different ways. Pressure makes it better. Do not avoid it—embrace it. Many acts base their decisions on their comfortableness, instead on their professional interest. However, carefully assess your decisions in terms of utilizing the opportunities that you are being presented with once you are in a position to clarify your goals and how such decisions can affect them, since every single action can have major consequences, which can affect the development of your brand. In order to be in a position to fully utilize and take full advantages of the chances for career growth that you are being presented with to your benefit, it is important for you to strategize your moves without any personal feelings or emotions reflecting on your rational thoughts. In other words, you will have to be able to very often neglect and overcome any strong personal feelings, opinions, and prejudices you have toward certain individuals and circumstances if you want to ensure that you are capable of capitalizing on every situation that you are being involved in. It is important to say that, although sometimes you will have to ignore and overlook the emotional effects, which some interactions and cases are presenting you with, this does not mean that you have to forget your perceptions and notions and change the way you feel. If you have something to prove, do it. Utilize and recognize your feelings and transform them as motivation to succeed, but do not use them as a base for your decisions.

Results Take Time

Never expect quick and immediate success gratification, because if you evaluate the efficiency of your actions based on this approach, you would be often frustrated and not satisfied with your work due to completely irrelevant reasons. The main principle behind every single piece of action and operation in the music business favors the quality, not the expediency, of your activities. It is about achieving the right result, not the quickest one. The direction is always more important and valuable than the speed. Do not rush. Impatience is your worst enemy, because it favors time over quality. You should avoid the chance of being negligent to the details of your activity due to being concentrated on meeting deadlines, whose importance is unreasonably fixed only in your perceptions. The music industry is not an activity field that can offer you fast and immediate career development and results, so you should be aware that the lack of patience is definitely not a trait of your character that you would like to be associated with and exploit over the course of your professional activities. You should make sure that you are hungry, driven, and yearning for success, to possess the ambition to put all of your capacity and working potential in the process of working toward your goal, but you should also make sure that you are looking to achieve the right outcome, not the quick one, with your actions. There is a huge misconception about what exactly the term *success* in the music business is formed by. Unlike previous periods, where popularity was definitely another word for success, the situation in the current state of the entertainment business is not in a position to certify and confirm such statement anymore. Nowadays, the possibility of achieving popularity in a short span of time, relying on factors and circumstances that are not necessarily dependent on your profile, is still quite a realistic outcome, considering the fact that the way the music is being perceived by people can still generate a significant amount of exposure, if the consumer is being presented with a quality product. However, it is also safe to say that popularity is not something that can guarantee profitability and sustainable career, unlike before. Hence, sustainability is not a matter of high-quality product showcased in the right circumstances, being at the right place at the right time due to luck and fortune. It is a matter of professionalism and hard work, consistently applied to a career throughout a long period of time. It is not about intensity; it is about consistency. But it is mostly about an intense consistency—the ability to perform your respective actions and advance with your development in the highest and most efficient tempo possible over the longest period of time. The rate of your enthusiasm and drive to succeed should be constantly high and you should not let the time to have any negative effect on it. The positive outcome is a result of steady progress and perseverance to the whole process and not episodic efforts. It is very similar to the process of going to the gym essentially, for example. You cannot expect that you will achieve significant progress with your body transformation as a result of one training session, regardless of how intense and productive it would be or how dedicated you might be to it. The bigger the volume of work and the bigger the amount of time that you spend on your working capacity on are, the better and more impressive and sustainable the final results would be. The same principle applies to a career in the music industry as well—you can devote all of your money, time, and passion in your career over a short period of time, but the truth is that the positive results are a product of a long-term, constant commitment, not of chaotic, unorganized, and unstable outbursts of motivation and transient drive for success.

Sustainability over Popularity

It does not mean that you are rich if you are popular, and vice versa. Exposure and popularity does not necessarily equate to income. The high performance of your brand in one of these aspects of your activity is most certainly a step forward to improving your progress in the other one; however, each one of these areas should be treated separately, with different approach and mentality. Achieving popularity and ensuring a sustainable income are two fundamentally contrasting tasks that you would never be able to complete according to your benefit if you expect that one method would provide you with the results that you need in the two fields. Learn how to treat and utilize your success from every single perspective if you want to construct the fundaments of a career, which can satisfy not only your personal desires, but your common human needs and requirements as well.

Goals Prioritization

Construct and develop your brand to a sustainable, respectful, and prolific name in this business, concentrate on your long-term goals in favor of your short-term ones, and carefully and strategically allocate your efforts in order to maximize the rate of your efficiency. Long story short, choose quality over quantity and invest your work in promising opportunities and projects, instead of aiming to achieve quick, but temporary success, by unnecessarily overloading your working potential. It is important and of significant meaning for every artist to be capable of rationally assessing the characteristics of their product and to use them to their benefit in the process of setting realistic and reasonable goals that are pursuant to their current development stage.

Stay focused on the end goal. Do not mistake progress with success. It is completely reasonable and understandable to be excited, enthusiastic, and delighted once you see that the efforts that you are investing in your career are being justified and you are achieving growth in your activities. However, such developments are not to be misjudged as success. An artist should clearly understand that such positive results are only an expected course of action, whose purpose is significant only in the sense of pursuing your final, ultimate goal. Allowing temporary positive results to change your predetermined mentality and outlook on your professional activity can have a crucial effect on your work, so an artist should always accept the pleasant results generated in the process of approaching the final stage of their planned success with restrained positivism. You cannot let yourself feel satisfied. You should be satisfied only with the thought of chasing satisfaction and with the concept of always improving your current status and accomplishments. You can never afford to be complacent or indifferent toward your activity. When achieved after relentless work and dedication, success can be incredibly overwhelming to a point where it can significantly cloud your already established perceptions and judgments to a level where it will damage your further career development. It is very hard for some people to maintain healthy mentality and correct psychological approach. Every single successful endeavor that you undertake should be assessed as just a step to another one.

Remember that you will never achieve success if this is the essence of your actions. You will never receive and generate attention if this is the main thing that you aim to get. Do not target attention when it comes to creating your music. Your one and only goal should be to express yourself and genuinely enjoy and cherish the opportunity to use what you are in the process of achieving what you want. Once you start valuing the success of your actions based on the attention that people are providing you with, that is when your efforts with this will become less and less efficient and irrelevant. Do not try to impress people with your music. Try to impress yourself with it. And do not feel bad if you notice that your enthusiasm and passion toward your actions are not shared, appreciated, or understood by the audience at some point. You should never let such reactions make you belittle yourself and undermine your satisfaction of fulfilling the desires of your essence.

Dedication to the Process

Success is a natural process that you cannot fast track. One thing should happen before another and you cannot skip stages to directly reach the final one. The big results happen once you realize that it is all about the culmination of small progress that you have generated throughout your professional career. Short cutting means that you are short cutting your potential and the opportunity for you to showcase and cultivate the full range of qualities and features that your profile possesses. There is no tool that will do something that you cannot or transform you into something that you are not. There is no shortcut, no easy way for doing things. You are more than welcome to try and aim to fast track your development, but you can be certain that you are most certainly not capable of short cutting it. The nature of the business and the community is such that hard work and personal approach are the words that are capable of ensuring progress. Do not make exceptions and do not tolerate underperformance. If you set standards related to your work, efforts, productivity, or advancement, you should always make sure that you will complete them correspondingly. Do not make excuses or try to convince yourself that you have a proper and actual reason and excuse to not deliver the results that you have promised yourself to generate. If you, for instance, have decided that you will contact 100 promoters per day in the process of booking your own tour, you should do so and the fact that one day you have experienced lack of energy and dedication to do so cannot justify the fact that you have contacted just 50 of them. Let your work and actions describe your value, do not rely on words to do so. Excellence speaks for itself. Essentially, everyone can claim and say that they have produced great and high-quality results, but the people who have actually achieved it do not need to promote their accomplishments further or in a hyperbolic manner. It is very easy to produce low-value work that meets common standards, but the main goal is to generate rare results that only you are in a position to achieve. When undertaking a certain endeavor, the artist should understand that every piece of activity's main purpose should be not only focusing on achieving the final destination of the said operation, but also acquiring and developing professional and personal growth by expanding the artist's knowledge, experience, expertise, and qualities throughout the process of completion of the said project. Every career move should not be perceived just as an opportunity for expansion from a business perspective, but as a chance to learn and extend the potential of your talent and professionalism. Hence, underlining the need of having a learning curve associated with your activities, as well as the chance for meeting your career goals, is the approach that should be utilized when it comes to choosing the professional opportunities to take advantage of in the process of developing your activity.

Understandably, it is very difficult to note what and how you should do in order to improve your chances for achieving a successful career in the music industry. You should rather first determine what and how you should not do, rather than the opposite. Obviously, creating a high-quality artistic product is a common sign for success that every well-performing act is familiar with. Due to the complex nature of creating such overall effect, however, it is extremely challenging to list all of the aspects that an excellent, effective product can be associated with. However, it would be relatively easy to mark all of the points that you should avoid in the process of creating it. Moreover, every artist should be aware of the concept that success very often is not a matter of achieving and working toward certain aims, but also subtracting elements of your activity with negative effect on their career. When it comes to appearing dysfunctional in a certain part of your overall performance, you should be able to recognize when it would be better to not try to overcome the problem, but to simply remove it instead. Trying to build a well-operating career is quite a challenging and difficult task to be completed, and aiming to do that while carrying burdens and problems of different nature in your bag is not only a method that lacks efficiency, but such that can significantly damage your performance in the long term; hence, it is important to not indulge in any operations and procedures of achieving a goal, if the characteristics of your profile contain problems that might act as an obstacle and hinder the success rate of your actions. If there is an issue, address it immediately. Neglecting problems will not make them disappear, so you have to be sure that you and your performance are in the best possible conditions to generate positive results before launching the procedure of achieving them.

CHAPTER 5

Developing a Strategy Is Important Only If You Are in a Position to Fulfill It

While a fixation on results is certainly unhealthy, short-term goals can be useful developmental tools if they are balanced within a nurturing long-term philosophy.

—Josh Waitzkin

Career strategizing is an absolute necessity in the process of establishing a stable career in the industry and a powerful tool that can precisely narrate and guide the progress of the professional growth of an individual, but only if it is rationally and reasonably developed, in accordance with the artist's specific characteristics and goals. Strategizing, planning, and organizing your career are the natural processes and steps that an artist must undertake in order to fully complete their ambitions for success in the business. However, a vast majority of music acts tend to not understand that conceptualizing their activity matters only if they are in a position to implement, execute, and perform their developed thoughts in reality as well. Hence, when approaching the strategizing process, every artist should set realistically established goals and points that can actually be fulfilled and beneficial to their respective activities according to factual and objective considerations, rather than working toward aims that they want, but are not capable to fulfill. The strategizing process, ultimately, gives you the chance to construct your elevation to success. It is a complex and sophisticated procedure, which requests an incredible amount of maturity, rational thinking and approach, and knowledge and natural understanding of performing certain operations. You can proceed to establishing your development strategy only once you have a set goal that you want to achieve, as the said plan should be built in a reverse order and fulfilled in a step-by-step manner. Strategy should not be a visual presentation of the ideas you have in mind, ordered in a chronological order, but a guide to the actions that should be undertaken in order to achieve the completion of the respective steps that are noting your career path. The segmentation of the different activities performed by your brand should be carefully allocated to their essence. Do you want to improve the monetization of your profile's activity? Do you want to achieve exposure? Do you want to work toward developing the creation of your identity as an artist? Ideally, every one of the aforementioned aspects should lead to the establishment of positive results in the other two as well, forming a steady chain and flow of activities. In order to achieve progress with your career, it is important for every action and activity related to it to have high level of conversion. Every positive result that you achieve with your doings should lead to improvement in every field of your career. Assess and observe the tendencies of your activity and carefully analyze what aspects of your performance deliver exposure and what part of your profile's operation is responsible for generating profit, for example. It is unlikely, especially at the early stages of your career, that you will find a unique approach that will be capable of providing you with positive results in these two areas simultaneously, so it is crucial to understand this principle and utilize this knowledge in the process of establishing your plan of action and strategizing.

Sequence of Actions

The worst possible move for a formation to undertake a process of achieving a desired result is to try to directly progress from the starting position to the desirable outcome. The process of approaching a goal should be divided into as many small steps and check points as possible. This methodology automatically encourages the attention for detail in every single operation and provides every single step with the awareness and the focus it deserves. It also gives the artist the opportunity to more easily allocate the right amount of effort and mindset to each action, which ultimately creates a very cohesive chain of operations with good flow between them, eliminating critical risks and stress levels. As with every other endeavor of complex nature that a person should deal with, the best method to approach a complex procedure of completing a sophisticated task consists of breaking every step of your strategy to little pieces and ensuring good and convenient progress flow between the respective activities. Overcomplicated moves are never beneficial and efficient, but quite the opposite, as a matter of fact; hence, make sure that you are committing to a process that would be easily apprehensible, understandable, and comfortable for you, if you want to put yourself in an environment where your potential would be utilized to its maximum capacity. Ensure that you are in a position to approach your plans. The method that a musician is undertaking toward the strategizing process of fulfilling a goal, to a large extent, can predetermine the efficiency and the success rate of his or her actions; hence, it is preferable for an artist to understand and make sure that the procedure of attacking the certain task is planned and organized in the most logical, applicable, and smart manner possible, pursuant to the specific end aim.

Objectives Accentuation

Every professional goal that an artist is aiming to achieve should be measurable and scheduled, so the process of approaching its completion can be monitored, revised, and strictly followed in order for the artist to be capable of noticing tendencies and principles that are affecting the positive progress, which should be considered and, eventually, exploited as well. Every action should possess a performance indicator, which can help you to track the effectiveness and the performance of the certain endeavor. Efficiency is an extremely important and underrated term, undertaking a crucial role in pretty much every aspect relevant to a career in the current stage of the music business. The amount of achieved opportunities by an act is falsely glorified as an important standard, while the feature that doubtlessly matters is the percentage of positive generated results by an opportunity. It is all about the artist's potential to properly take advantage of the chances received and extract the results needed for the development of their pursuant goals. For example, when it comes to digital marketing, using the modern online tools and the opportunities for receiving insights regarding your activity provided by the different social media and streaming platforms gives you the opportunity to track and follow the number of sales that your music is generating and compare the results achieved through a certain period of time; the sort of content that is most effective in encouraging sales, traction, and exposure; the demographic groups and the target audiences that are most active in terms of consuming the body of your work; and more. When a goal is defined and clarified using the aforementioned criteria, the next step would be developing an action plan explaining and mapping the process of achieving the said goal that should contain activities in the different components of an artist's activity, which might be relevant to the specific goal, including, but not limited to, promotional methods, advertising, content creation, social media performance, networking, branding, touring, and so on.

Selection of Priorities

Nevertheless, your activity should be unpredictable and your audience should be always looking forward to your next move in terms of your career path. Every move you make should have a purpose and the ability to meet multiple objectives. When constructing, planning, organizing, and performing your marketing activity, you should ensure that you are in a position to use every single promotional opportunity to its full capacity.

An artist should be cognizant that one action is not necessarily meant to serve just one purpose. To the contrary, in order to improve the efficiency of your performance levels and guarantee the maximum results that you are capable of achieving, you should be able to validate that one piece of planned activity should be suited to meet multiple different purposes and tasks at once, especially if you want to truly maximize and capitalize on your profile's attributes and talents.

Dealing with Disruptions and Complications

Meanwhile, an artist should be aware of the concept that—regardless of how much careful planning and strict organization are being implemented in the process of completing a strategy for success—there is no way to prevent unwanted and unfortunate turn of events, and they would need to, eventually, face and deal with unexpected, sudden, and uncomfortable situations, which do not correspond with their personal preferences, in terms of actions. Hence, it is important for an artist to anticipate drastic changes and unforeseen problems and develop the ability to adapt and act in such a quick, accurate, and smart manner, as things will rarely happen exactly as planned. In addition to that, an act should understand that it is needed to be able to work and modify the circumstances that they might find themselves in to their benefit and always be in a position to control the narrative of the particular situation accordingly. You might not be capable to command the nature of a certain occurrence to your preferences; however, you must always try to avoid acknowledging your eventual impotence or inability to control the characteristics of the eventual problematic state, especially when it comes to cases involving multiple parties, where there is a chance for your reputation to be hurt and your brand to be damaged. It is easy and normal for a musician to experience frustration, disappointment, and dissatisfaction once a huge investment in terms of time, money, and emotions is being made to an operation that does not unfold as required and expected. However, a principle that the act should utilize in such situations is that sometimes there is not a problem if you do not acknowledge that, specifically when it comes to your audience. For example, you have promised and you have been heavily promoting a new release on a certain date; however, you understand that this would not be possible due to a last-minute issue faced by your distribution company, for example. As unfortunate as that is, this is nothing to panic about and it is certainly an event that your fans do not need to know about. If you provide further details and information, you will only damage your brand and put focus on the issue that the majority of your audience would not have even noticed otherwise. Have you seen the biggest acts in the industry nowadays discussing in details and explaining themselves why certain things haven't occurred as announced and expected? Exactly. Essentially, people do not perceive such technical situations as too serious, so you should not too, because, objectively speaking, an artist is not in a position to rationally decide what the magnitude of a situation truly is and sometimes following your emotional opinion can only blow a problem out of proportion completely unnecessarily, only causing problems, instead of avoiding them.

SWOT Analysis

The SWOT analysis is one of the most well-known planning methodologies that is, as a matter of fact, incredibly applicable to the artist's development aspect of an act. The concept behind the SWOT matrix is based on the exact approach that a musician should undertake in terms of self-assessment and gathering the needed information out of the aforementioned process needed for the creation of a proper strategizing procedure. An acronym for strengths, weaknesses, opportunities, and threats, this analytical approach provides the artist with the opportunity to correctly and objectively extract information about their essence and implement the generated conclusions to the artist's action plan that should underline the career path of the act. The SWOT approach is a very comprehensive and easily accessible tool for a performer to understand their respective strengths and base their activity around the idea of emphasizing on them, note the weak aspects of their activity that should be improved, and research the characteristics of their target business field in order to recognize what would be the most rational and efficient way for their profile to exploit and take advantage of the present career opportunities, to avoid an eventual failure and damaging results and outcomes. Every professional artist should remember that they need to adapt the analysis to their career and avoid adapting the specifics of their activities to the SWOT analysis instead.

Strengths

The information related to the artist's strengths discussed in a SWOT analysis could be in regard to the different aspects of the respective music industry participant's career—from a creative and business perspective. The unique talent of the act to create a high-level product; to provide and deliver unmatched in intensity and quality live performance; or to possess noticeable aesthetics, which are peculiar and attractive enough to generate noticeable interest from the mass audience, are possible features that can mark the exceptional level of a creativity of a content creator, while marketing potential, capital collaboration with experienced and proficient industry professionals, the ability to operate in the current state of the industry, to be able to note and take advantage of the active tendencies in it and achieve high level of monetization, can be listed as aspects that showcase the professional, business awareness of a formation. In general, every trait of a profile, which exposes the value of high potential to be hardly matched by the majority of the competitors in the industry, can be considered as a general strength.

Weaknesses

Inability to write, create, and record good quality of music or perform live; absence of creativity and desire for innovation; deficiency of funds and financial investments; lack of support from people with high expertise could all act as potential weaknesses of a brand. Market saturation and the incompetence to deal with it could also be a major and significant problem, considering the negative effects and damages that can be caused by it, due to lack of knowledge, understanding, and information to apply to an activity in such circumstances, as all of this leads to a noticeable deficiency when it comes to support from secondary markets as well. Lack of ambition and drive for high level of success could also be a weakness of a great scale in the long term.

Opportunities

Overall, opportunities can be considered as the development and establishment of niche markets, specification of target demographics and customer segments, freed marketing shares by competitors, new tendencies provided by the development of the culture, or the technology advancement of the tendencies in the business and the constant new options and platforms, which the music industry environment is exploring and developing nowadays. Every aspect of the entertainment sphere that has the potential to generate career growth in one way or another should be considered as an opportunity, regardless if it can be classified as a common one or not.

Threats

Any factor that possesses the potential to interfere the process of development or a planned plan of action and cause an unexpected turn of events should be considered as a threat. Commonly known as risks as well, threats include potential tendencies that could require the unplanned need of additional investments for the completion of a certain operation or that can lead to decrease of the chance of certain moves and ideas to achieve positive results. Such can be presented specifically by the way that the online platforms are operating nowadays, considering the constantly changing key performance indicators and requirements that the said platforms' algorithms present to their users in a very sudden manner, which completely modify the approach and should be undertaken in the process of utilizing the advantages of the said platforms.

Phases of Content Release

There are three main phases forming the general schedule, which a release process should follow in order to improve the certain artist's progress and product exposure:

- Phase I—the beginning stage of the promotional procedure. Phase I's objectives include achieving significant brand exposure through the specific content release and generating traffic toward the artist's profile, in order to build stable media platform for extended content reach. Phase I consists of concentrating on generating the biggest possible attention to the specific piece of promoted content and attract as much attention and traffic with the first release off the eventual promotional schedule, in order to construct a better platform for the upcoming release plans.

- Phase II—the culmination of the commenced process. The main purpose of this phase is increasing the attention to the main objective of the undergoing project through activity aiming to improve the purchasing behavior of the audience and increasing the conversion and efficiency of the promotional processes, as Phase II is the stage where the presented content should be used to extend its reach to new audiences, demographic groups, and market niches and expand the brand's activity to a larger amount of target audiences.

- Phase III—the final stage of the defined campaign, which should transit the generated positive results and momentum to the next planned activity off the previously created action plan. Phase III is responsible for utilizing the achieved through the previous stages of exposure and traffic and implementing the generated results to the process of further extending the artist's brand exposure. In its nature, this stage is an ongoing process, where the discussed releases should be used as a tool to complement, promote, and draw attention to all of the other respective artist's endeavors (tours, merchandise, and so on).

Ideally, Phase I starts with the release of the specific content and the launch of the promotional process for it, as Phase II should start once the publicity processes for it are over. When generating features and articles during the strongest moments of the promotional campaign, it is crucial to make sure to share these features on your professional and personal platforms as well. You might not be used to that or you may find this unnecessary, but this activity actually is of significant importance. Every share generates traffic that massively raises the presentation efficiency of the said product. After Phase I is completed, you will have to adjust your actions to the specifics of Phase II. The activities that you will have to perform might sound very similar to the one in Phase I; however, you should be aware of the difference in the concepts—during Phase I you are aiming to attract people to the created product. During Phase II you have to bring the product to the people, which means that you have to change the dynamics of your actions and work differently on the separate channels that the said content is being presented on, so strong social media performance is, again, essential here. Phase III is quite self-explanatory. The main point that you have to perceive here is that you have to intersect all of your activities in one cycle, where each participant in it leads to all of the others. This is the phase where you use the potential and the momentum that any of your actions has developed in the process of improving the performances of your other endeavors. Put merchandise links and information about your upcoming shows on your YouTube videos; when on stage, performing live, tell people to watch your video; when sending merchandise, include a note saying that you have upcoming shows; and so on. In order for this configuration of activities to be capable of performing high-quality and brand-defining results, it is crucial for the artist to clearly understand the nature of the different phases and the respective processes and fully commit to their correct exploitation.

CHAPTER 6

Do Not Follow Tendencies—Create Them

Go your own way, don't imitate.

—Nikki Sixx

The entrepreneurial nature of the music industry is such that it always endorses and encourages uniqueness, creativity, and personal touch. The key principle that should be realized and recognized about the process of achieving certain goals is the fact that the construction of a fruitful business activity requires certain steps to be fulfilled in this cycle. However, many participants in this sphere follow the wrong impression that such steps should be completed in a certain pattern as well, which is not corresponding to the reality of the situation, in any shape or form. Not only this is not the case, but, as a matter of fact, acts and professionals who choose to approach their specific plans using their own personal perceptions and self-developed methodology will always tend to be exposed to bigger amount of interest by the music community and, respectively, achieve and generate more significant and positive results. The question that must always be asked when a development strategy is about to be performed is not only what the desired goals should be, but, most importantly, how such goals will be targeted, reached, and completed.

Lead, Do Not Follow

Defy categorization at any stage of your career development and work against the concept of being described with common terms and characteristics. If the general audience is in a position to put boundaries on your profile, this means that you have done the same to yourself as well. Uniqueness is not something that can be described in a standardized manner; hence, you should be aware that if people try and manage to put your product and career under already developed perceptions, you need to strive to change that. Be different and create your own market. Relish the role of being an innovator. You should not be creative only when it comes to your art, but when it comes to your business as well. Essentially, an artist should escape from the perception and the understanding that they need to shape their career according to the current market's requirements, if they want to be successful. While this is always an option, a musician should not be afraid or ignorant of the possibility of establishing their own market, their own unique niche for development. You do not always need to follow rules, tendencies, and popular trends in order to achieve certain accomplishments. You can create them. At the same time, it is also an enormous mistake to follow such concept if it does not feel natural to your personality and your certain mentality. There are no certain rules to follow; you just have to make sure that you are following your very own intention and process of development that is most suitable to your distinguishable characteristics and features.

Embrace Your Uniqueness

According to Einstein, the definition of insanity is doing the same thing over and over again and expecting different results. Having said that, the idea that you can follow a specific development pattern and apply the ideas that your competitors are utilizing with their respective activities to your career and expect to be better than them is completely ridiculous. Do not associate yourself with a certain movement or popular trends. Being connected to a current strong-performing and well-developed tendency endorsed by the music industry and hailed by the audience can be an approach that lots of artists might be very tempted to undertake, considering the potential of such move to deliver fast, easy, and addictive amount of positive results to a career. However, in the long term, lack of identity, creativity, and desire for genuine and personal touch is not a quality describing success. Embrace your uniqueness. Follow your gut. Many acts tend to falsely assess their personal, unique trait as an aspect of their career that would need to be modified in the early stages of their development in order to suit the industry requirements, which they believe are crucial for achieving success. It is easier for an act to fall in the trap of concentrating on building a common, conventional profile following an already established path, rather than shaping their own, personalized approach, considering the lack of confidence, knowledge, and understanding of the nature of the music business in the early stages of a brand development. You cannot form and shape the characteristics of your activity based on a pattern or on an already defined formula. The truth is that the task of identifying what sort of presence and qualities the mass audience appreciates and likes in an artist is actually way more difficult than most of the people think. It is extremely wrong to believe that the qualities that you see in a formation are the same that other people admire and, respectively, make the said act popular and successful, so it is very inaccurate to base the development of your actions on perceptions that might not be entirely true. As a matter of fact, the audience does not base their decision to like, follow, and support a musician based on a certain aspect of their career or personal character. People are attracted by the nature of the whole product that they are presented with, not the different parts and components that are forming it, essentially. Having said that, that is the reason why following the idea of giving the fans what you think that they might want to see and hear from you is a very inaccurate strategy to utilize in the process of achieving success, just because you cannot really know what people exactly like and prefer, since they do not have a particular and well-explained opinion on this too. Fans are drawn to a product based on its overall quality, uniqueness, and charisma, and developing a well-operating and interesting brand is not a checklist procedure that you can complete in a conventional manner. However, introducing your distinguishable character and unique personal approach in a drastic manner and trying to convert all of your unusual features in a marketing product that is dramatically different in comparison with the common requirements of your respective part of the industry would be unlikely a winning formula too. You have to determine the tempo of the flow, which you have to utilize in the process of exponentially and gradually forming and arranging the characteristic features of your product to be presented in a cohesive and comprehensible way to the end user, where the final impression instilled will be emphasizing on your peculiar traits, but the said effect will be achieved through taking advantage of practices that can ensure a positive perception by the end consumer. Adjust successful and well-performing tactics to your profile and goals, not the opposite. It is very much understandable and reasonable to follow and utilize the tactics and the strategies that artists of a higher level use in their respective endeavors. However, you should be aware that replicating the methodology that a certain act is taking advantage of would not necessarily reproduce the results generated by it when applied to your particular case as well. Having said that, make sure to not shape and form the characteristics of your brand to the requirements of the certain method that you would like to extract results from to an example. Rather, make sure that you are doing the opposite—adjust the specifics of the method to your unique brand traits. An act should always follow and keep attention on the successful patterns and approaches that other participants in the music industry are utilizing to their benefit and use the gathered information in their own respective activity. However, it is crucial to understand that in a market and business where being unique and possessing peculiar approach and profile are requirements for success, you cannot expect to be better than anyone if you are just repeating already exploited tactics and do what everyone else has been doing.

Fundamentally, every development move is a very complex procedure, and as everything in this business, it is quite impossible to successfully undertake such operations by following a palpable pattern. There is no winning formula; every step and action should be pursuant to your specific goals and the results you want to achieve with this whole process. Hence, considering and discussing your essence as an artist will help remarkably to build the concept in your mind that you should follow throughout your career. The key question to be successful in the music industry is not where you can fit the piece in the puzzle, but rather what the piece's form should be. Have a direction, and be yourself. Due to the uniqueness and tendency of entrepreneurial approach and innovation being rewarded when it comes to achieving positive results with your activity in the music business, it would be very naive and unjustified to believe that an already used pattern and utilized formulas would get you the desired progress once applied to your current case. Moreover, as already discussed, every step that an act undergoes should be pursuant to its specific strategy, profile, and goals. A certain approach proven as successful for one artist can be not only not useful, but also damaging if another act with completely different characteristics features and aims decides to utilize and take advantage of it. Synchronization is a key, and careless approach when it comes to forming your decisions on questionable information and perceptions can achieve great misbalance to the efficiency of your actions, ideas, and goals.

CHAPTER 7

Understand Your Audience

Being an entertainer includes knowing how to connect with an audience.
—Joe Nichols

Understanding the people that a brand is meant to target is the first step to attracting them and is the main point described in this chapter. Following the behavior tendencies of an audience and gathering data regarding their preferences, as well as utilizing this information in the process of promoting content are key features to extending the reach of a product's activities. The music business is so incredibly and fascinatingly influential and successful because, unlike other industries, it satisfies the end consumer's needs in a variety of different aspects by providing experience that influences a person's senses in multiple distinctive ways, unlocking feelings and perceptions, which cannot be generated or substituted by any other product. In its essence, the concept of the music culture is so appealing to the mass audience because it does generate and create a landscape of a community and a sense of genuine belonging to the end user.

Comprehend the Process of Connection

Influential and successful acts are such due to their capability to create and offer a product that is an irreplaceable commodity for their respective audiences, making their status and presence such that cannot be substituted by any potential alternatives. The process of targeting is not defining the general specifics of your audience only. Certain artists tend to believe that once they receive some ideas and notions about the overall characteristics of the people, who they see during their shows, or the ones that interact with them on their social media accounts, they start to understand and have an in-depth knowledge about their audience and how to approach the procedure of targeting. Which is, to some extent, correct; however, nowadays popularity is based on social currency. People enjoy the feeling of being identified and associated with their interests—this activity of indirect interaction with their favorite musicians or artists gives them a sense of purpose, belonging, and the opportunity to establish a bond with something or someone that they feel close to. Having said that, when it comes to the process of connecting your activity to your audience's attention, an artist's goal should not be to necessarily and only establish a fan base with their product, but to provide this kind of a value of social currency, which people are looking for. For instance, people who enjoy sport love to expose and showcase their fandom and their admiration to their favorite athlete or team. They do love wearing their favorite player's jersey and items that expose their level of affection to the said person or brand. Why? Because these sorts of actions are increasing their social currency and help them to think that they are perceived by other people in the way that they want to be perceived. This same concept is fully applicable to the music world. Once you determine what sort of content that you are capable of producing have the potential to make your audience feel proud and satisfied to represent your brand, you will know how to use your talents and intrigue people with your work. This is the ability that will help you to extend the reach of your actions organically, and that will increase your social rank. You have to understand your audience, the principles behind the activity performed by the people who follow your career. Why do they like you? What do they like about you? How they perceive you? How they expose their support to you? Gathering data and information about the way that your fans interact and invest themselves in your activity, utilizing the extracted knowledge from such operations and forming, organizing and performing your actions in accordance to the established tendencies is the only method that can provide you with the opportunity to exploit the support of your fans to its highest possible level and generate the results, which you might need from this field of action in order to achieve career growth. Even from a personal point of view, you have to be willing to understand how people perceive actions and respect and consider their notions in the process of building your professional level.

The Big Wins Come with the Small Ones

Attracting one fan matters, and spending significant amount of effort to do so is not irrational. Building a fan base, to a large extent, is basic and simple mathematics. It truly is a game of numbers and working toward exponentially organizing your audience growth as a mathematical progression. As such, in order to expand the reach of your activities to as many people as possible, you have to start your efforts from the first, lowest progress step—gathering the attention of one person. Contrary to popular belief, the sustainable way to establish a profitable and well-operating career is by developing your profile and audience from the first level of exposure, step by step, slowly and steadily, before progressing to do so globally, even though the advantages of the social media platforms can suggest differently. Even from a personal perspective, an artist would be more beneficial to steadily develop understanding about interacting, engaging, and establishing audience on a smaller scale, rather than getting involved in operations that would require more experience, knowledge, and intuition. Many artists find the incentive to do what they do only once they see the possibility of achieving significant, almost unnatural progress. However, undertaking such approach is actually one of the most unreasonable decisions that a formation can take advantage of. Do not aim to impress the mass audience at once. Try to base your efforts on getting the attention of each person separately, at the same time. Treat the people following you as a community, but aim to showcase that you do not perceive them as one universal massif, but as a combination of different individuals, where you appreciate their personal characteristics and notions.

Expectations

Do not aim to meet people's expectations—aim to exceed them. An artist should develop a mentality where, regardless of what the exact situation and specific requirements are, there is always a desire for adding a final touch to the respective activity, which would doubtlessly impress the final user and would put your action over the top in terms of the generated effect. Attention to detail is a necessity. Aim to create an impact. Possessing an influential value is the asset that can guarantee long-term stability and sustainability in terms of your product and career's performance. Whatever task you are performing, invest 1 percent more effort and passion into it. Make sure to reach your absolute limit and then surpass it. If you believe that your career is worth pursuing, then it is worth putting an extra effort in it as well. Give away more than you receive. The way to utilize the marketing potential of your audience to its full capacity is by providing your followers with a value that is on a higher level than the invested time or funds in return. This is how people would be interested in your activity and overall performance—by understanding that they are profiting and receiving more from this interaction than what they would with another artist. Once a person realizes that their efforts are appreciated and acknowledged better by you than your competitors and that you treat your audience with more care and attention than your market rivals, this is where your approach would create a long-wasting, sustainable, and positive impression, which would start defining the performance of your brand.

Give the people what they want, but do it how you want it. Yes, the essence of the entertainment industry is quite simple in its structure—you will be in a position to generate beneficial results with your activity once you build a methodology that can provide the audience with the product that they want. However, they key point to this aspect and principle is

regarding the fact that while you need to consider the audience preferences and desires, you have to comply with their requirements in the way
that you want to do it, not how you think people would like you to do so.

The Focus of Impression

The biggest and most noticeable problem that many young artists struggle
to recognize and address is the lack of proportionality and cohesiveness
in the different aspects of their promotional work, when a part of their
careers is not representing their overall vision as an artist. You might be a
group producing great music, with very active live presence and already
establishing a stable fan base, yet your online activity might not be representing the potential that you are able to offer in these areas at all and you
have to make sure that you are in a position to level that. Yes, you are generating interest from people, you are being involved in good interaction
with fans that like your music, but here is the key thing—you should not
aim your activity to be noticed by people that are already aware of you,
that are already hooked to your product and will follow your progress.
You have to work to get the attention of those who do not have any idea
of who you are and you need to develop the constant urge and ambition
to expose your music to people outside of your reach, all the time. It is a
matter of perception, but as you know, the internet is providing you with
the biggest and most efficient tools to get your profile popular. And the
beauty behind it is that you can count only on your efforts and activity to
achieve that, at least to some extent. So, make sure to promote your content constantly. Many people tend to worry how this sort of actions and
attitude are being perceived by the audience in general and they do not
want to establish themselves as click-baity working artists, unnecessarily
exploiting methodologies with questionable effect, but thinking like that
is a common mistake, which will only prevent you from extending and
showcasing your activity to new people. After all, you should be receptive
and appreciative of how much you are putting in your respective career,
so it is only natural to make everything possible to show your product to
new audiences as well, as there are a lot of people out there that will love
your music and product. However, at the early stages of your career, no
one will seek your specific activity and products, so it is your job to put

them in front of the eyes of the audience that might be interested in following your professional progress.

Professional Landscape Overview

Audience Profile

Main interests and subinterests and the establishment of a general audience profile can be determined through gathering information about the following aspects of your audience's profile, which can provide you with the chance to not only understand but also know the people that you would be in a connection with through your music. Following, considering, and utilizing the main characteristics of your audience and implementing the formed conclusions in the process of building the specifics of your marketing activity can have a crucial effect on the positive rate of the execution of your business strategies and approaches. Collect knowledge about the aspects that are constructing the profiles of the people who show tendencies of appreciating your activity, such as general age, gender, type of personality, behavior, secondary interests, consumer tendencies, other favorite artists, preferred social media platforms, and approach in terms of exploiting them. The ability to construct a legitimate and truthful impression of your audience and its preferences, features, and attributes will give you the chance to better know how to use and shape your own talent and activity in order to form a better, more sustainable, and long-lasting connection with it.

Analyze Your Market

Even if your strategy does not include synchronizing and shaping the nature of your decisions in accordance with the established business sphere of the activity of your competitors, you should—at any stage of your career and development—be in a position to be cognizant of the circumstances that your career is being involved in and be aware of every industry aspect, which have the potential to be relevant to your career at some point. Follow and study the most successful acts in your scene—both local and global—and consider the utilized approaches and methods, which they are undertaking in the process of achieving exposure, engagement, and traction. The generated conclusions will help you to evaluate the eventual reasons and decisions that might be preventing you from generating the best possible results that your potential might be capable of and find better and more efficient ways of utilizing your talents in order to determine accurately the buying potential of your products, the active tendencies that can maximize the ability of a product to score better sales rate and to define the most useful, helpful, and beneficial promotional content that you can use for the exposure of your product. Moreover, receiving in-depth and detailed idea and perception of the following topics will confirm whether the field of your activity and career sphere that you chose to participate in is capable of providing you with the opportunity to construct a sustainable, successful career.

CHAPTER 8

Develop a Band. Represent a Brand. Marketing Is Everything

Although capacity may be oversold, you can never oversell the product. You can always continue to sell the goodwill and the assurance of quality and service that make buyers seek out your brand beyond all others.

—Paul B. Buckwalter

The most important truth that you should know about the marketing process is that it is not difficult and you should not be afraid or intimidated by it. The best marketing is simple, and it covers complex and sophisticated duties, using plain and straight forward approaches. Marketing is not a process with a fixed duration. It is an ongoing operation, which requires constant configuration and adjustment, as well as attention and strict approach in order for the artist to be in a position to generate the respective results that they might need for the particular stage of the career that they are currently undertaking. Marketing is the component that connects the artist's music with the right audience. You might be exceptionally talented and unique with your craft, but only marketing can bring your qualities and style to people's attention. In order to be successful, your marketing activity should have a purpose and a specified goal.

Define Your Own Aesthetic

It is essential to understand the importance of being honest and genuine to yourself, as an artist, a performer, and an official business participant. When working on the image of your activity, the main purpose is not to portray yourself in the way that you think people would find you interesting and intriguing, but to find the comfort zone and the characteristics where you are in a position to honestly and truly feel comfortable in expressing your individuality to its full extent to the mass audience. The way a formation appears not only in front of the audience but also in front of the music industry in general is, arguably, the most important factor for success. Respect is received only if it is earned, and the way a product is represented is the way that it will be perceived. You have to be proud of what you are doing and be satisfied of the opportunity to be in a position to present it to other people. You should be passionate about it and be excited about the chance of your audience being excited about it as well, because if you are presenting content just for the sake of it, everyone will be, eventually, able to see and sense the lack of honesty in your actions, and this will have a fatal impact on your career. Essentially, the audience is subconsciously always attracted to sincere attitude and the pure character of your activities and talents, so if you would like to involve yourself in the complicated process of establishing an emotional connection with different people, you have to make sure that you are exposing the full specifics of your persona to them. Music shares the characteristics of essence with every other form of art and contains the concept of a noticeably abstract configuration to portray and convey the artist's personal and emotional essence and acts as a vessel and an artistic embodiment. You should be willing and ready to gather the main core of your individuality and the essence of your vulnerabilities as a person and expose them to the audience. To showcase your desire to establish a deep and meaningful emotional connection by undertaking the first step of the process of developing a unique, safe psychological environment that all of the people who choose to be associated with your career and art would be capable of utilizing in their personal endeavors. Delivering a high-quality product that is aiming to attract personal attention is just the first step of the process. But you must be aware of the fact that you should not concentrate on providing your fans with a chance for them to be involved with your talent in certain occasions only. Develop a culture, an immersive appearance, where the end-consumers would need and strive to bond the characteristics of their lives to yours. Your very own unique vision and its respective characteristics should contain exceptional and unparalleled traits that can be perceived and defined by your audience almost instinctively. The people that would be exposed to your product should be able to feel and sense your presence and style, rather than experiencing the need to think and require further explanation in order to actually understand what your vision truly is.

Attract the Desirable Attention

Aspire to keep the consumer constantly interested—the progress of your career should follow the principle of the development of a book, movie, or a song; in other words, every action that you undertake should aim to offer progress and evolution. You should always aim to generate a result that would be viewed as abrupt by either the industry or the audience. As a creative sphere, the music business is a field where you cannot afford to act in a traditional and safe way with your endeavors, and you should avoid at any cost structuring an activity that would be easily predictable for the consumer. You should make sure that there is always suspense and interest to what you do, and you can only achieve this by putting a lot of thought, concept, and genuine passion into the process of planning the steps of your development. Once you start making, creating, and doing things based on your concerns, rather than on your talent and intuitive ideas, people will start noticing and sensing the direction of your actions before you are in a position to even fulfill them. If this happens, naturally no one would be intrigued by what you do, since they would already know the characteristics of the thought process that your decisions are based on. It would be illogical for a person to follow your journey and career if they already know what the end results would be and what and how you want to present. Be unpredictable to yourself. Let the flow of your creativity dictate your moves. Only such an approach would lead to a natural and genuine career progress and creative process in which you can not only participate but also expose to the people that you would like to attract them with your actions. Do not try to intrigue people to follow your career; instead, aim to take them with you on your creative journey and in the process of achieving success. Do not perceive them as viewers but as participants in your move to conquering the music world. Add value to your presence by being perceptive and intuitive to the way you are interacting with the people who are interested in your endeavors. The main purpose of your promotional activities from a business perspective should not be necessarily making your audience to enjoy your content; instead, it should be about making these people interested enough in your activity, so they would have the desire to continue following your actions in the future. The motive of a project should not be to generate maximum attention to it only, but to make the end-user visit your previous actions and anticipate your upcoming ones. Predictability is your enemy, so you should avoid being monotonous or repetitive with your decisions and moves, regardless of how successful they might have been in the past.

Brand Development

The key to establishing a successful and well-operating brand and career in the entertainment industry consists not only of creating an unique and remarkable product that a large number of people would enjoy and ap-preciate but also constructing an overall appearance and characteristics of the said product so that every fan would experience the genuine need to expose what they are associated with to their eventual clique. Determine what your unique selling proposition is, that is, your specific trait, your weapon to impress audience and to garner attention to yourself. Your career will become successful once your music transforms from content to culture; only then you will be capable of influencing your listeners in multiple ways and you will be appreciated as a figure with its own specific features, rather than a simple content creator. Once people start realizing that your activity is something peculiar and exclusive and being associated with your brand would be a choice that could lead to improvement in terms of opportunities related to social interaction, social status, and popularity, your overall appearance as a professional act would elevate from a brand with the potential to generate interest to a phenomenon that is capable of influencing mass audience, as this will be the moment when industry professionals of any kind and level would notice you and would note the benefits of collaborating with you. This will lead to exponentially growing opportunities for success.

Presenting and showcasing a brand is not necessarily about who you are at this particular moment; rather, it is about who you will become eventually. The development process should not be directly associated with cultivating the artist's present qualities but with completely reinventing its characteristic features and profile and, possibly, unfold a whole new aspect of personal skills and traits that would expand the respective brand as well. Most of the times, young and inexperienced acts have the tendency to involve themselves in the psychological cycle of perceiving themselves as one-dimensional entities and basing their understanding on the illusions that they have developed from specific life experiences in the past. An artist should always remember that their quality is being showcased through their current status, not their previous accomplishments. Your profile is not defined by who you were, but by who you currently are, so do not let past decisions control your future ones. It is about what you will do, not what you have done.

Chain Activity

Your promotional activity should form an endless chain of actions that have the capacity to gain and maintain the attention of the consumer, maximize their interest, and capitalize on it. It is of significant importance for a brand to be able to convert the generated attention to stable results. Considering the very impatient and demanding behavior of the consumer in the very overloaded music industry, being efficient and able to fully take advantage of the time that someone is allocating to discovering and appreciate your product is essential. Therefore, it is important for every artist to make sure that they are using a continuous promotional scheme that contains a chain of activities forming one cycle of operations leading to the different aspects of the artist's career, where there is always a next step and action to undertake, without any dead ends. Do not neglect the element of presenting yourself. Use your profile and platform to present your music, but do not forget to use your music to promote your profile. Every operation that is related to your activity should not be a one-way process, but rather a part of a procedure where the potential of your efforts will not be exhausted once it reaches the end-user but will be relocated to another aspect of your respective operations. Your activity growth should be organized in a continuous process. The key to structuring a well-operating brand only goes through the proper allocation of your personal qualities and their correct implementation toward completing an artist's specific plan. The development process of an act should not be considered as a variety of different procedures acting separately in their respective fields but as a synchronized effort aiming to achieve a cycle of simultaneous operations where each action is dependent on the progress and can have an effect on the other aspects.

Develop Your Own Marketing Niche

Do you matter? Does your activity have a significant impact and influence on your audience, peers, and industry? What would change if you career suddenly stopped? Would there be a gap that would form if you stop doing what you do? If an artist is not in a position to determine specific answers to the aforementioned questions, they should very seriously reconsider the purpose and the essence of their activity. When trying to exactly locate and position your appearance in terms of career significance, you should be aiming to undertake a crucial role in the already established configuration of the music industry and avoid undertaking a complementary or secondary position that does not have a clearly defined and meaningful participation in your specific field of action. Try to establish yourself as a profile that would create a massive gap if you were to cease activity—one that the rest of the participants in your field of action would like to fill immediately if the right opportunity arises.

Your art is not about making a record that is most saleable, but creating music that is honest, genuine, and pure. Stay true to your artistry, but modify your career. One of the biggest misconceptions that many artists experience throughout their professional endeavors in the industry is being incapable of properly distinguishing the different aspects of their activity and properly allocating their mentality to them. A considerable amount of acts struggle to find the balance between their craft and the business of presenting it, which generally is something an artist is obliged to do in order to assess and connect every action with the right, effective method. An artist should be approaching their art genuinely and naturally, but they should be dealing with their career strategically. Your career is about presenting your art to the general audience through delivering a product that has the greatest possible potential to encourage traction. The popularization of the branding of a product is a complex procedure that is necessary to be executed through the relevant channels and platforms and utilization of every sort of promotional tools in order to be fully successful. Initiating a purchase is a very different process in its nature in comparison to initiating someone to attend a show, for example, which requires to be approached in a different manner and style in order to achieve successful results in the end. The aforementioned concept is more than applicable to the different types of content that you career is producing as well. Strategizing and performing your promotional activities in accordance to the specifics of the separate types of products that you are creating, your current status, and your short- and long-term goals is a much-needed method for your career growth. However, an artist should understand that such external methodologies are only complementary operations and do not define the true nature and essence of the branding concept. While it is impossible to complete the process of successful branding without taking advantage of the opportunities for exposure to the mass audience and the industry in general, an act should understand that the branding of their act is truly an internal process in its nature that the artist should first deal with, design, and clarify before undertaking the stage of seeking exposure through executing the said process. Marketing activities can maximize the potential of your product, but they cannot improve it; therefore, it is essential to ensure that your profile is at its peak phase before going any further with your actions toward promoting your productivity.

Business Diversity

Always embrace the constant changes, innovations, and newly introduced tendencies that mark the evolution of the music business. Lots of participants in the music world tend to automatically resist their adjustment to such changes and speak against the specifications that modify the cycle of actions that they are forced to adapt to. This indicates a major flaw in terms of mentality and mindset when it comes to utilizing the characteristics of the music world to your benefit. In reality, every change, every new adjustment, provides new channels and opportunities for growth that can be exploited only to the artist's benefit. If the music industry is evolving and moving, you should do too.

Spread your activity and work on as many different projects as possible. The more seeds you plant, the better is your chance to grow something. The more content you produce and showcase to people, the bigger your chances are to get noticed. In other words, never put all of your eggs in one basket when it comes to your career and be proactive with developing new ways to achieve your goals—establish new methodologies, utilize different tools, innovate your approach to your daily activities. Do not try to earn money and collect a budget from just selling your music—try to improve your monetization levels by promoting your merchandise, collaborating with brands, looking for outside investors, offering lessons, and so on. Use product placement in unexpected placements. Very often, the biggest earning potential for an artist is not necessarily related to their music, and an act should be fully aware and mindful of this idea in order to efficiently utilize and take advantage of their brand's profit capacity. The additional income levels needed to not just meet your financial needs but to actually start generating stable profit could be only acquired through extensive and unique marketing approaches, where your activity will not be focused on just your predetermined, optimal marketing niche and demographic groups but where you will be capable of using every single promotional opportunity to your benefit. Do not promote just your music—promote every aspect of your activity as one whole, homogeneous product. More often than not, the general audience bases the decision to show interest in an artist on the overall presence that a profile creates, not just a single aspect of it. Aim to make your audience feel your music and presence, not just listen to it. Use as much working potential as possible in your marketing. Regardless of how well-trained, proficient, knowledgeable, and capable you are to perform the promotional activities related to your profile's career to the highest possible level, your capacity would never be enough to meet the needs of your act to evolve in terms of marketing.

Social Media and Digital Marketing

It is of a significant importance to study your audience and the behavior of the people that you want to attract to your product and utilize the generated information to your benefit by synchronizing your actions to it. Taking advantage of the opportunities that the newer trends in the industry offer—in terms of modern platforms, social media, and so on—is absolutely required as well, but, once again, the key factor to strong promotional performance is setting the right goals.

The social media platforms are not just a tool that you can use to improve your career and overall brand performance anymore. You probably already know how important, crucial, and essential your performance and activity are in terms of network promoting in order to satisfy the music industry needs nowadays. However, the trends emerging in the business recently showcase a new narrative—the social media will soon become not just an important side of your career but the most essential and crucial part of your promotional activity that will completely change the established dynamics and patterns that have been in existence in the music business in relation to music release, promotion, and so on. The whole concept and principle of hiring PR companies for promotional cycles, for example, is losing its efficiency, and, possibly, it will become completely irrelevant in the music industry at some point in the future. Of course, using this kind of pattern and practice is sort of a must to follow if you want to achieve and generate a certain amount of exposure. Nevertheless, it is getting progressively outdated, and very soon investing in such projects would not be a rational and cost-effective method to gain attention to your product and improve your career. This is just the natural progression and evolution that the industry is going through at the moment. Even now, press opportunities are mainly providing creditability rather than exposure. The whole music business, like every other industry, for that matter, is getting more and more reliable on social media performance, and it is important for every band to adapt to this trend and fully embrace it. No one is really looking for new artists and music on outlets, especially the younger generation and the demographic groups that an act needs to attract. New music is being discovered on YouTube, Facebook, Instagram, and Twitter, and it is really rare to meet someone who still buys magazines and visit specific websites to find new music.

The Algorithm of the Platforms

Every major social media platform is based on a different concept and supports nonidentical practices that are most suitable to the said platform's characteristics. In order to achieve the best and most efficient results with your online activity, you have to respect and work with the specific features that each platform possesses in order to exploit and utilize the advantages created by the performance algorithm constructing the behavior of the online client.

Recently, crucial and significant changes have been added to this concept of social media promotion, which is an extremely important detail and something not to be neglected or overlooked. These recent amendments will completely modify the dynamics and the base of the operations involving promoting content on social media, and it is important for every participant to adjust and adapt to this idea in order to not only keep their actions to a level where they can produce normal results but actually utilize these new opportunities that they are getting to a positive end. You will have to treat every type of content differently, depending on the platform that it is presented on, rather than trying to synchronize all of your activity in one big chain of social media performance. Seek guidance and assistance in terms of exploiting the advantages that the social media platforms can provide you with in terms of developing and marketing your brand, expanding your marketing position, extending your reach, and targeting a wider audience in the current music business environment. Considering the fact that your social media efficiency is of critical significance now, it is safe to say that if you want to succeed, you have to focus on this aspect. Understand how platforms and tools work. Do not hope for the best results; make sure that you are in a position to achieve them. Engage and gain traction. In order to generate the results that you are expecting to get, you have to persistently follow the right moves. Undertaking one step and neglecting another would achieve nothing.

The most crucial components that you should consider in order to make your digital marketing activity successful are persistence and consistency in your actions. The key to establishing and forming a stable social media audience that can get you progressive growth in terms of exposure is setting a trend that you can follow. It is not important to create and present content frequently, and the key aspect you need to consider is that your uploading schedule should follow a certain routine. Uploading and presenting products chaotically would not generate the results that you are expecting, no matter what sort of content you are presenting. Having said that, the first thing that you should do is to work on forming an action plan and pattern to strategize your uploading schedule around.

Regardless of how effective, useful, and successful your approach toward the usage of the digital marketing strategies might be, the exploitation and the utilization of the social media platforms is an aspect that should be constantly improved. You most certainly should start presenting and promoting more content on your accounts, as personal accounts are included as well. It is essential to understand that a crucial part of a strong social media presence is developing and utilizing the potential that your own online presence and profiles possess, so make sure to develop your personal activity alongside your professional ones. It is also important to do all of this—preparing posts, sharing them with your fans, and interacting with them—and you will generate successful results only because you have experienced the genuine urge to do these activities and not because you feel that you need to do it, just for the sake of it. The general audience is very intuitive—people can easily sense, even subconsciously, if the content presented to them is delivered as a commitment. And if they feel that you are not investing the desire and passion into interacting with them, they would not do that too.

Consistency and Conversions

Due to the opportunities the Internet and the modern digital tools are providing in terms of promotional activities and user experience nowadays, a piece of content created by an artist could be exposed to a large number of people who are in no way related to your audience or its specifics. Hence, a crucial asset for an artist when it comes to the digital marketing area is to be capable of efficiently exploiting the generated transient traffic. An action that can be very damaging for your brand and the efficiency of your overall performance is leaving dead ends with your actions. Every piece of content or action that you produce should be linked to the other results of your activities in order to form the previously discussed promotional chain. When you release a new video, make sure that it includes your website that, when visited, displays information about your upcoming shows. Once the webpage containing your shows appears, it should refer to your new merchandise. When the user browses your merchandise, your website should redirect them to your social media accounts that are promoting your other songs and so on. You should confirm that everything is tied together in order to navigate the traffic from one place to the next. However, it is also necessary to acknowledge that in order to get the best results you should not overload the attention of the end-users with too many options and opportunities for redirecting their potential as consumers. Putting all of your links and promoting all of your products at one place would not fully engage a person, but in fact create an effect that is quite the opposite. Their interest will be wane, and they will likely abandon your pages instead of exploring them further. Numerous steps with minimum options is the most interactive, engaging, and useful method to showcase the full prospectus of your product to your audience, rather than trying to expose at once everything you have. Create different contents to promote different products.

Artist-Based Marketing

Considering the unpredictable way that the most used platforms are constantly changing nowadays, it is crucial to explore and develop different marketing methodologies and not count entirely on the services of platforms that will only require you to pay more and more to use their services to full extent with the time. Artist-based marketing is evolving even now, so you will have to start building the foundations of an alternative way of online promoting immediately, if you do not want to find yourself in an unfavorable situation in the future. It is highly likely that very soon all of the popular social media platforms will start exploiting your dependence on them to their benefit through raised prices for paid advertisement. That is their main idea, to navigate your efforts in centering and building all of your activity on one place and then start profiting by asking you for more and more money, in order for you to be capable of utilizing everything that you have built, because they know that you do not have a second option. You either pay or you lose your results and progress. Just think about how dependent your career and activity are on the social media platforms nowadays, for example. How do you think your profile will be affected if any of your current online pages are unusable? If the answer is yes, this should give you an indication that you should start developing a conversion between your different profiles and find different ways to be in touch with your audience. Therefore, it is important to simultaneously start establishing your own platforms while making sure that you are generating the best possible results out of the opportunities that the social media websites are offering you right now—divide and conquer. It is all about engagement over visibility. Bringing interactions from third-party social apps to artist-owned platforms like email, text, and events give the artist more control and better return of investments overall. Direct fan communication beyond social media typically yields stronger results, in addition to being more cost-effective than wasting budgets at promoting social media posts. In addition, considering the ongoing debate of how many ad clicks are fraudulent, an artist-owned platform that requires more consistent real-world interactions is a better system for tracking both the quantity of human interaction and the quality behind those engagements (through sentiment analysis, etc.).

The Principles Forming the Efficient Advertisement Process

An inevitable part of the procedure of fully exploiting the advantages of the social media platforms to your career's full benefit is acquiring the knowledge and learning how to correctly utilize the opportunities for paid advertisement that the said tools are providing their users with, especially when the topic of the activity is related to the entertainment industry, where the ability to reach as many people as possible and present your activity and the results of your talent to as greater audience as possible is one of the most valuable and efficient performance indicators for establishing a well-performing career in the music industry nowadays. Due to the constantly changing nature and environment of the digital advertising process, the continuously evolving regulations and requirements that the clients of such services need to consider and the incredible amount of variables that need to be clearly defined, explored, and noted in the process of adjusting and modifying an advertisement process to a particular case, it is impossible to develop a quick, universal solution and methodology that can always ensure positive results, regardless of the case, and which will need to be implemented in operations such as data gathering, monitoring, and analyzing for identifying relationships between variables, forecasting outcomes, mapping events to trended data and findings in order to develop a working and efficient algorithm to follow, as this is a topic of information that would require a separate body of work to be explained, described, and presented properly in its entirety. However, while the method of approaching the process of paid advertisement is not something that can be showcased in a brief manner, the principle of the approach that should be adopted in order for positive results to be delivered is actually about following a few simple and essential steps that can ensure establishing the right frame of actions that will lead to positive outcome if implemented effectively:

- Defining the nature and the focus of the end goal through specifying the desired key performance indicator. The right advertisement campaign requires a clear idea of what your motives are (achieving traffic, brand exposure, or sales-driven results).

- Correct and efficient allocation of budget. Bigger investments to small target preferences is the way to move forward in terms of constructing your campaigns, in order to maximize the exposure of your activity and get the best level of return of investments possible.
- Exploring and considering multiple targeting features and consumer behavior is an absolute must. Ensuring the establishment of direct, unambiguous objectives with your campaigns is necessary for your overall return of investments. The smaller your target is, the higher your efficiency will be. This is the stage where the artist should utilize and take advantage of all of the gathered information and details that they have regarding the specifics, characteristics, and traits of their audience in order to find the most efficient and useful arrangement for defining the right target for their advertisement process.

CHAPTER 9

Value Your Time. Respect Your Work

It's all right letting yourself go, as long as you can get yourself back.
—Mick Jagger

Work Reflects on Health, Health Reflects on Work

Although the overall common perception might not suggest this, there is actually a noticeable difference between the operational approach required in the entertainment industry in order for positive career progress to be achieved and the regular working specifics of a typical, standard day job. Each market segment has its own specific characteristics and requirements that the respective participants must comply with in order to ensure positive career growth. When involved in the music industry, a person is investing their time and efforts in order to generate results, rather than simply fulfilling a certain role's requirements. It is the ultimate application of the quality-over-quantity principle. As such, an artist cannot afford to perform their respective activities automatically; every action requires maximum dedication and attention in order to deliver the preferable final product. The consequences of such a working dynamic are substantial; the exploitation of the artist's capacity to its full extent is an exhausting process, both physically and mentally, and for the sake of the final product's quality, the artist should be aware and always appreciate the fact that their condition has a considerable role in the creative and professional cycle of a career in the music industry. Hence, the ability of a person to understand when to take a break, relax, and rest is much needed, as they will never be in a position to create the best possible product that they are capable of designing when they are not in the best possible condition. Overworking is never a solution, so you should learn the specifics of your limits and understand the importance of unwinding and giving your body and mind a chance to rejuvenate, so you can recharge and be ready to take advantage of your full potential once the right time approaches. It is likely that once you get yourself involved and get used to a heavily loaded cycle of activities benefiting your career, you will find it harder and more difficult to not spend time working on your progress, but in such situations you just have to remember that performing activities while you are not in the proper form to do so is only a waste of time and effort. Therefore, always make sure to take a break and give your body a chance to restore its full power when needed. Do not compromise your health for results, because you need your health in order to generate the results, which you should be aiming to achieve. Due to the incredibly overwhelming amount of personal commitment required for an artist to develop and maintain a sustainable career in the industry, you should make sure that you are always preserving a healthy mental health state as well. The levels of stress or anxiety that you might be facing on a daily basis can significantly damage your self-awareness, creativity, and drive for success, and moments of this sort are the periods when a person is most vulnerable and allows unrealistic fears to negatively influence their mindset. This is why you should always find time to give yourself some rest and the opportunity to spend time in peace; ignore your fears and trust your true intuition, so you can ensure that you are in the best possible condition to reach your full potential when it comes to taking advantage of opportunities that can eventually advance your career.

Sustaining Motivation and Overcoming Fatigue

Getting to the successful level is easy, but sustaining it is hard. Contrary to popular belief, gaining attention and interest from record companies, managers, booking agents, press, and receiving opportunities for expansion through them does not mark your success in the music industry. It actually indicates the launch of your actual career in the full meaning of the word. There is a common misconception that getting recognized, noticed, and provided with the opportunity to dedicate your time to a full-time career in the music business is the largest obstacle to be tackled for an artist on the path to success. While this stage of development is indeed incredibly challenging, difficult, and hard, an artist should be aware of the fact that their career only actually starts when they get the chance to step on the highest possible platform, because the only thing harder than establishing your brand and associating it with high standards is maintaining this status for a long period of time and sustaining the high production value of the product that you are generating. Releasing four strong singles over two years and performing highly energetic shows while your eyes are strictly and most concentrated on your goal is doable, but nourishing constant motivation and drive to keep doing what you are doing following the highest possible standards can be a very draining and emotionally exhausting process that you might not be able to keep up with. The worst thing that can happen for an artist is to see their goals achieved and expectations met. Fulfilling your goals and desires could be actually one of the most strenuous and hard concepts that an artist might be in need to adjust their mentality to, considering that such turn of events completely changes the dynamics in an act's career path and mental state. Hence, it is important for an act to be anticipating such turn of events and, apart from the rational goal for achieving success, to work toward an ongoing desire, such as self-improvement from a personal and professional stand point, which is a flexible goal that cannot be affected by any external circumstances and outside situations related to the artist's career and can be used as a guiding light for progress once the other circumstances surrounding the artist's career cannot act as an incentive for additional personal and professional growth.

The music industry provides a strongly unstable and rapidly polarizing gradient of evolution and progress to its participants, which often places the artists in situations of radically different nature. Dealing with such hard-to-predict circumstances often can have a very negative impact and influence on the artist's mentality due to the sudden and stressful changes that might occur to a career unexpectedly and that require immediate action and consideration. An act might find itself on top of the world at one point and then experience an overwhelming career fall right after that, which is a very complicated and challenging concept to get used to and familiar with; hence, an artist must possess the ability to anticipate this sort of developments.

In order to do that, there is one principle that every performer should always consider—the highest and strongest point of every act's career comes after their worst one, and that is why only the personalities that possess significant persistence and strong will to undergo difficult experiences at some point in their career find themselves successful at the end of the day. You cannot let your guard down. Failures beget obstacles, and success beget obstacles in the music business. Therefore, you are not in a position, at any point, to not be aware of the circumstances or the situation that you are in. The music industry is extremely inconsistent when it comes to the growth of your profile; you can reach the highest highs and lowest lows in one day. Your biggest success might come just after the worst point of your career; however, the opposite is highly likely as well; you can hit rock bottom right after you have thought that you have achieved the success that you have always been working for. The better your career is developing, the more significant the magnitude of your actions will become; therefore, you have to be extremely self-aware, cautious, and careful, because—regardless of where you are with your career—there will always be obstacles and problems that might have crucial and dramatic consequences if not approached in the most careful manner possible. Nothing is guaranteed. It does not matter how well or how poorly you do in this realm; everything can change in a second, so you should be thankful every single day about the position that you are in and treat it with respect, attention, and professionalism. You have to live with a sense of gratitude, because in an instant everything can change.

Value Your Accomplishments and Work

Follow and appreciate your progress. For the sake of your creative state, mentality, and motivation, you must always make sure to occasionally determine and assess the positive results that you have managed to generate with your work and appreciate them. Considering the hectic and intense routines that a well-performing act should commit to in order to be in a position to produce improving and beneficial results for their career, at certain times it would be very difficult to properly appreciate and evaluate the level you have reached. It would be easy to minimize the tempo of your progress, which is a prerequisite for experiencing a significant amount of satisfaction and fulfillment leading to a decrease in the levels of drive and enthusiasm that you have to put in your efforts in order to become successful. Simply try to cease your activity for a moment on a regular basis and observe your career, actions, and results not from a subjective point of view, and you will be amazed to learn of the progress that your hard work and dedication have achieved while you have been immersed in the process of approaching and completing your plans. Do not overthink and spend your energy on revisiting past situations or worrying about future outcomes. Do not overanalyze. Concentrate totally on your actions at this particular moment, because only they matter. Thinking about consequences is thinking negatively. Sleep and take care for yourself. Never let yourself, your life, productivity, and well-being be a victim of stress. Stay healthy to be productive. Be productive to be successful.

CHAPTER 10

Communication Matters

To effectively communicate, we must realize that we are all different in the way we perceive the world and use this understanding as a guide to our communication with others.

—Tony Robbins

The Merit of Communication

The music industry environment presents a very unique business landscape, where success is a reachable destination not only if you are in a position to create leverage through unique, high-quality product, which can be responsible for brand expansion, but if you are also capable and willing to develop and effectively exploit the specific quality to cooperate with other professionals and the audience, in general. The eventual significant results that you can possibly generate with your activities, talent, and work would never matter if you are not in a position to showcase them to the professionals or the people that would be interested in them. You should always respect every single individual who has offered and provided you with help of any sort. Regardless of what your status is as an artist, every success that a music act generates is based on other people; this is how the music industry and the music community work. No matter how good you are, you will never be able to progress with your actions if there are not any people to listen to you, journalists to report your activities, audience to attend your shows, and, of course, associates to support you in your respective endeavors. No one owes you anything. You should understand that no one, whether we are talking about the general audience or the participants in the music industry community, owes you attention, appreciation, or admiration. You have to earn and deserve those, and, in order to do so, you actually owe the people who are in position to improve your act your full respect and gratitude for even just providing you with the slight chance to gain their interest. Always be thankful for the attention you get, because although you might deserve it, in this day and age you are not in a position to insist on it. This is why networking is an integral aspect of an act's activity, which might be, arguably, the most important procedure that you can be involved in, as your communication approach matters more than you can possibly imagine. It is crucial to understand that only respect begets respect, and regardless of what the situation and given circumstances are, you will receive the attitude that you showcase. Make sure that you treat everyone you meet with equal respect, regardless of what the status of the people you interact with is. Never let ego get in the way, because your ego represents your personality, not your brand, and these are two opposites that should never be conflated.

As previously mentioned, a significant part of being a participant in the music world is to be also a valuable member of the industry's community and endorse and support the progress achieved by your competitors in their respective endeavors. Being in good terms and praising other acts for their work and results is essential, not only because your brand would be responsible for the positive evolution of the culture of your sphere, but because—in the context of the constantly changing nature of the music business—you also never know which artist that opened a show for you would be the next big event in the entertainment sphere. It is very likely and possible to acknowledge and notice a certain strong tendency during the time of your experience in the entertainment industry, which is the fact that the more prolific, respectable, accomplished, and well-known the professionals that you might have the chance to cooperate alongside are, the better, more respectful, genuine, and kind will be the manner in which they would treat you. Big, successful, and accomplished musicians and industry professionals are not nice, kind, trustworthy, and reputable because they have achieved their goals. They have achieved their goals because they possess the aforementioned qualities. People often misjudge that success shapes personalities, which is, actually, an applicable and correct statement to an extent, but it is important to note that in general the unique characteristic traits of a person and a musician are a factor that shapes their progress and success in the music business.

General Approach

In an industry where success strongly depends on the connections that can be established, your approach in the process of utilizing those connections and the way a profile presents itself, treats, and communicates with the professionals around it can generate opportunities never imagined before. Respect, professionalism, kindness, and a personal touch represent the method that should be adopted with every message, email, and phone call produced by an artist in the process of undertaking duties seeking professional growth. Always strive to be transparent, honest, and honorable. The music industry operations are based on people with very strong and significant profiles, characters, and egos. Sometimes, something that initially seems to be a harmless situation of not providing ancillary, pointless details in order to save time might lead to creating a significantly tensed environment and trust issues, so you have to showcase your personal value to everyone you are working with or are aiming to collaborate with and expose the value of your ethics, moral, and principles in order to be in a position to build the fundaments of a positive and productive cooperation.

Decide why you want to work with people. Is it because you want to utilize their qualities and knowledge and form cooperation that would be beneficial for your career? Do you need people who you can trust and would be able to provide you with a constant emotional and moral support? Do you look for an experienced team that possesses proven expertise and qualities or do you want a highly motivated and driven but young group of people that genuinely believe in your qualities and career and are ready to do the impossible to provide you with the results you want? The truth is that either choice has the potential to generate amazing progress and meet your high expectations, but only if you decide to go with the option that shares the same mentality and vision as you do.

Understanding people—their reasoning and the meaning behind their actions, thoughts, and emotions—is a quality and approach that should not be neglected in any way. Respecting the people that you collaborate with and their intentions from a business perspective is most certainly a strategy that can improve your chances to establish a fruitful and beneficial working environment that you can capitalize in the long term, but the ability to invest effort in the process of getting yourself familiar with the specific features of the people you are working closely with can be the foundation upon which you can build doubtlessly a sustainable personal connection that is a significant prerequisite for building a professional one. Understand that everyone has a personal life and experiences that affect their professional relationships and activity, and this is why communication is an universal solution because it gives you the opportunity to accurately understand and assess the specifics of the situation that you are experiencing and use this knowledge in the process of determining the most rational and efficient decision, given the particular circumstances. Aim to understand how people feel and think, before trying to understand how they work, because only utilizing empathy and personal approach in terms of your communication is the way to be in a position to develop and maintain high level of useful and mutually beneficial connections that your career undoubtedly needs in order to progress.

Communication with Industry Professionals

When trying to arrange and accommodate an eventual collaboration that your career can benefit from, do not try to use your motives to request such a partnership as your main goal. Rather, explain why the other party should be interested in cooperating with you. An experienced professional can assess whether a received query is worth being considered and if an opportunity might be promising by the way the idea is being presented in the first place. The main purpose behind established music industry parties to consider cooperating with a certain act is that they believe such a collaboration will improve their status and will offer them a chance for growth. Hence, when undertaking the process of establishing a dialogue with an entity that you are being interested in being associated with, you have to be clear in terms of what you can offer them, rather than presenting yourself as another formation that just wants to be accepted as a recipient of opportunities in an eventual partnership but is not capable of giving anything in return. Show your value and potential, expose what you can do for a business, and do not just submit yourself, hoping to get a gratuitous role.

Bulk emailing, cold calling, and using the same template in the process of contacting business professionals and seeking opportunities for your career is the worst possible approach that you can utilize in this area of your activities. There is no palpable pattern that can ensure positive results when applied to different cases; however, there are some specific principles that you should always and undoubtedly consider once you feel that you are in a position to embark on such activities. First, an intelligent approach to your verbal and non-verbal communication style matters. The way you structure your thoughts, present your questions, formulate your sentences, and comply with the common standards can show a lot more than you think to the person with whom you want to connect. It is about showing your potential to adjust yourself to standards, being capable of presenting yourself, and showing a good level of articulation toward your brand in the best possible way. Remember that music industry professionals do not decide whether they would work with a certain artist or not based only on the potential that a brand possesses for achieving mutual benefit and success. Most of the times, they would rather prefer to base their decision on whether you have the qualities to be a valuable and representable part of a well-structured working environment. Every professional party would like to be sure that they can trust you with their reputation once you start working together and be capable of not only appreciating, respecting, and complying to their standards, profile, and etiquette but also expanding their brand and helping them to progress in their respective endeavors.

Communication with Audience

Are your fans your family? Are they your friends? Or are they your supporters? You have to clarify what is the exact role of the people following your activities and base the type of the relationship that you would like to establish with them in accordance to your decision. Lack of synchronization between the different aspects of your career that concern the same group of people might be very damaging for your brand. Do you pretend and claim that your friends are your family, yet refuse to spend time interacting with them? Do you imply that they are your friends, but you are not in a position to commit to the sort of connection that such claim would require?

The ability to establish a memorable presence through developing a strong, polished, but genuine media profile and through general press appearance is another very strong tool that can provide you with many benefits, in terms of exposure, branding, and position in the industry, and, most importantly, it can help you to design a strong, natural connection with the people who are interested in your profile. Press exposure gives you the chance to showcase your character, personality, and specific features as an artist, in order to really show the audience that you differ from the majority of your competitors out there, even with your general approach toward such activities that are not necessarily related to your music. It gives you the chance to attract neutral members of the audience with your overall appearance that might not be impressed with your music otherwise. By putting the extra touch to your attitude and media presence, you indirectly show that you care and value how the fans perceive you, and this is something that most of the people would appreciate, even subconsciously, and would respond with the same enthusiasm that you are offering to them in the first place. Long story short, people would not give you the attention that you want if you are not willing to put more effort in this sort of activities and show them that their attention is important for you. Not to mention the fact that being able to generate good quality articles, interviews, and press features would mean that more outlets would be interested in collaborating with you, which would exponentially raise the level of awareness about your career in the music industry.

Communication with Your Associates

Acknowledging the specifics of the dynamics in terms of collaborating and working alongside your peers is the only way for all of the parties involved in the artist development process and for an act to be in a position to fully utilize and take advantage of their respective talents and provide opportunity for progress for everyone involved in such a partnership. You are dependent upon the productivity and the dedication of your team to be able to perform your respective role and duties at your absolute best. You have to be cognizant of what others need you to do as well. If you are in a team, you have to share the same mentality. Choose your associates carefully and demand the best from the people who represent you and your brand and whose work directly affects your career and success. Throughout your career you will most certainly have to cooperate and collaborate closely with different people and professionals in order to expand your activity and progress. Understanding the dynamics between the different characters that you work is a thought and a concept that should be strongly and carefully approached by an act. Depending on the specifics of their role, experience, and personal qualities, the different people that you might find yourself in a situation to collaborate with will probably have variety of diversified methods of work that they are used to utilizing in order to produce the performance and the results that you expect from them. Understand that in order to use people's talents and exploit them to their full potential for your benefit, the most rational thing to do is to give them a free rein in how they go about their work to produce the results you want. A smart and efficient decision would be to let people do their work in the most convenient method possible for them and to take advantage of their own understanding of performing certain operations. An artist should always make sure that they understand and are aware of how the operations related to their career are being fulfilled; however, it is also climactic for an act to be cognizant of what the different roles participating in the cycle of their career growth exactly entail and not interfere with their respective activities with unreasonable or unjustified preferences that can potentially harm the efficiency of the work that is being performed to your benefit, as the only party that would experience the negative outcomes of such damaged and unpleasant work atmosphere would be the artist ultimately. The true professional knows that the best way to benefit from a partnership with you is by helping your career to progress. The duties and the responsibilities of an official music business participant do not include performing operations in the way you want them to be executed. A professional's work is to achieve the assigned goal and produce the expected results, so the artist is not in a position to get involved in operations that are not relevant to their role and, most importantly, instill tension related to topics and activities that they do not fully understand. Trust your representatives and associates. The people who work for you, with you, and alongside you want you to succeed as much as you do. It is in their interest for you to progress and perform at the highest possible level because only then they will be able to generate good results, so you can and should trust their intentions, opinions, and methods of work.

Regardless of how talented an act is and how promising its career might become, people will be willing to cooperate with you and offer you the opportunity for mutual collaboration only if they see the qualities of a good team player in you. The ability to assess yourself, to work with other people, listen to and comply with others' advice; to be able to represent values that are not necessarily only relevant in this business sphere; and doing it all while you are genuinely pleasant to communicate with and to be around is one of the most essential and crucial skills that you can equip yourself with.

The Importance of Mediating

Learn how to mediate, since the ability to articulate yourself and communicate with people is very often the only method that can achieve a positive result in certain negative situations that you most certainly need to expect throughout your career in the music business. Do not shy away from dealing with serious problems, facing conflicts, and talking about the issues related to your career. Leaving problems unaddressed is the worst methodology that you can utilize, and such approach will only create bigger obstacles and problems for you to tackle and overcome with time. When it comes to embracing a professional conflict with a party concerning a mutual career-related situation, you have to understand that the purpose behind this sort of a conversation is to come up with a solution to benefit your work and profile by improving your current case without damaging the results of the work that you have already invested in the said project. It is a mistake of a significant magnitude to approach such a dialogue from a personal perspective and base your words, opinions, and reactions on your emotional urges. You have to understand that a personal argument is indisputably different from a professional one, and both of these require a completely different by nature approach, due to their radically dissimilar essence. The main goal that you should be trying to reach in the situations involving arguments on a certain professional matter is not proving your point of view and perspective necessarily, but gaining the maximum potential of the situation so you can benefit from it. In cases of disagreement, you have to present your eventual messages and views in a way that they will not be perceived as aggressive, offending, malicious, vindictive, or anything that is negative. Your approach and actions should not in any way encourage heated conversations, arguments, and bad feelings between the different parties involved in the dialogue, and every single delivered point and argument should be presented with utmost respect in order to avoid creating a personal conflict from a professional dispute.

CHAPTER 11

Be Careful, Not Skeptic

Begin noticing and being careful about keeping your imagination free of thoughts that you do not wish to materialize.

—Wayne Dyer

Caution Instead of Fright

Due to the nature of the music industry, there are plenty of frauds and self-proclaimed professionals with bad intentions that are using the enthusiasm and the emotional characteristics of talented individuals to their benefit, so many formations are—doubtlessly, reasonably, and understandably—being extremely cautious when it comes to cooperating with personalities, companies, and taking advantage of certain opportunities related to their professional evolution. While being careful is always a necessity, an artist cannot afford to miss an eventual chance that can elevate their career due to certain prejudices. You cannot develop a successful profile in the music industry on your own, under no circumstances, regardless of how exceptional your talent is or how impeccable your professionalism and qualities are, and you cannot advance with your professional standing if you tend to deliberately neglect or purposefully avoid opportunities for potential growth. Despite the exact situation and its characteristics—you have to know that there is a person that is covering your back. Regardless of how addicted and attached you are to the concept that you are the only person who can perform your career-related activities up to the required high standards, at some point it is necessary for you to find a way to rely on other people and be in peace and comfort with the idea of being dependent on someone else. Just think about this from the following perspective—there is not a single formation that has achieved success by managing and handling their entire workload. You need people. You need their enthusiasm, their working potential, and their trust, creativity, belief, and passion in order to progress further. The music industry is full of people that want to use you and benefit from you in one way or another, so it is important to be careful and understand the dynamics between the different operations in the business in order to avoid getting yourself involved in unfavorable circumstances. However, never be skeptical. Do not allow your fears, prejudices, or reservations to damage the progress of your career because only trusting and working with other people can provide you with the opportunity to achieve personal and professional growth to the level that you are targeting with your efforts. It is necessary to be cautious, careful, and precise when it comes to taking decisions connected to your career's evolution. You should always make sure that such decisions are not taken under any emotional or irrational influences, regardless of whether we are talking about positive or negative feelings. Interpret the signs correctly and learn to distinguish the people who are passionate to help you from the ones that are passionate to earn from you; develop and rely on your psychological understanding; and aim to comprehend human nature and ways of thinking when your activity depends on others. You have to want and feel that a working relationship would present you the results you are striving for, not merely hope that it would yield the desired results, and you should expect your prejudices to be defeated.

The Misconception about Mistakes

Mistakes and failures might be disappointing, but they are not damaging your progress in any way when it comes to the bigger picture of your journey to success. Undergoing setbacks, issues, and problems is an experience that can be easily classified as useful and helpful and incredibly beneficial for your long-term development as an artist and a person as well. Every negative situation has its own silver lining, and you can always count that the value of the learning experience that you can acquire from a situation that did not unfold according to your expectations might be more precious and important than if the opposite were to occur. Understand that every case, regardless of its nature, possesses its own advantages that you can learn and use them to improve yourself; therefore, you should learn to always extract the benefit out of the circumstances that you might be surrounded by. As soon as you acknowledge a problem or an issue, the possibility for change appears. Could you change the problem? Can you do it on your own? Facing issues is beneficial for your development, because it forces you to change and modify your thinking, to look at things from a perspective that you might not have been aware of before. You are in a position where the process of development of a skill or taking a decision is not optional and necessary and you cannot afford to put your comfort as a priority, but you should do what is necessary, regardless of whether you like the eventual resolution of the said problem or not. Such situations also can provide an artist with the most reliable information, which you can base your future decisions on—the personal experience. Doing mistakes actually might be an indication that you are moving in the right direction. People do not fail in endeavors that they are used to or comfortable with; they fail when they approach something new. Approaching new means evolution. Evolution means progress.

Yes, some chances contain the risk of failure that you might be hesitant to take, but they will most likely have the potential to help you progress and elevate your activity significantly. You do not need to feel ready, comfortable, or assured in order to take certain decisions that can ensure you a positive outcome eventually. In fact, experiencing such feelings of reservation and skepticism is only indicative that you are facing a possibility for expansion, considering that people are naturally unreceptive at first to situations, which require them to leave their comfort zone, as is something that an artist always should be willing and ambitious to achieve. In general, there is a common, well-known statistical observation that delivers a valid point—you will never hit your target if you do not shoot, so just do what you need to do, not what you want to do, and worry about the eventual consequences later, rather than focusing on them prior to their appearance. The habit of performing a preparation process preceding a certain activity is not always a beneficial method. Adjusting your mentality and mindset and equipping yourself with assets is required only when the success of the said operation depends on your preparedness, which, contrary to popular beliefs, is not what often the majority of people think. Most artists would choose to take advantage of an opportunity only when they are certain that they are in a position to approach it and when they believe that they possess all of the resources they need in order to do so. However, a concept that these people often neglect is that their perceptions are often not relevant and correct. In certain situations, you have to act fast. Sometimes, you do not need to achieve certain accomplishments, that is, to earn enough money, credentials, and connections and be completely comfortable, in order to make a move that can benefit your activity. You do not need to be ready in terms of your own understandings. You do not need reassurance, support, and persuasion to work toward a goal. Many people would not pursue their ideas and desires and perform their plans not because they are not capable of doing it but because they believe that they are not able to do so, which is a crucial misconception that an entertainment industry participant should avoid at any cost. If you cannot get over something, just go through it. You are not meant to always feel peaceful and comfortable with a situation, problem, or an obstacle that you are experiencing in order to overcome it. You just have to tackle it. Not to mention the fact that your approach in this area and in situations of this nature only showcases your professional potential and determination, and this is something that can massively increase your integrity within the music industry as well.

Fear and Intuition

An artist should be well aware of the difference between the terms "fear" and "intuition." It is a common mistake among people to misjudge the dramatic contrast between these two words, as the problems caused by the lack of understanding on the matter can be very harmful, damaging, and substantial when mixed with the highly emotional thought process that is related to the majority of the artists' characters in general. Hence, it is needed for every person interested in developing a successful career in the music field to be capable of properly identifying their intuition and fears separately and to be able to carefully draw borders between them, especially when it comes to utilizing the aforementioned feelings in the process of taking career-oriented decisions. As opposed to the essence of the fear, intuition does not have a negative presence and stressful effect on a person, but quite the opposite as a matter of fact. It provides the person with the comfortable feeling of certainty, based on previous experiences that might have been buried deep down in our consciousness. Intuition is actually a reaction that is way more than an instinct—it is the sense of a feeling, plus a rational consideration. Very briefly said, fear presents itself as negative emotion acting through different physical reactions. Meanwhile, intuition is the visceral guidance that a person receives subconsciously when needed. Fear is the negative feeling that urges a person to neglect their rational approach to life and to completely give up to their subjective preferences and concerns, by avoiding situations that present certain amount of unrealistic risks to the certain person, while intuition is the quality that helps you to see and assess a defined situation as it actually is and utilize your personal qualities, strength, will, and resilience in the process of overcoming the eventual negative outcomes. Developing opinions and expectations for the future based on premonitions is usually a beneficial methodology that an artist can rely on, considering that premonitions are generally neutral and extracted from the intuition. Premonitions are feelings that cannot be derived on purpose, as your subconscious thinking cannot reflect on their nature, which is the aspect that distinguishes them from the standard form of the fear. An intuition that is reliable and can be safely trusted by the artist normally contains information based on experience, not expectations—it acts on proven facts and impressions, not on emotionally established assumptions. A normal intuitive feeling is a positive, comforting sensation that supports your self-awareness and belief in yourself, instead of the opposite. The characteristics of fear are the complete opposite to that of intuition. Fear always expresses information based only on emotions and doubts, and it always causes stress, anxiety, and concerns that are the reason for harming the healthy condition of a mindset and, therefore, negatively affect the efficiency and the success of any operation or activity undertaken with such a mindset. An artist must be incredibly careful when deciding to base a certain decision on a harboring fear. It is most certainly possible for you to anticipate and sense a real danger at some point; however, in most of the cases, it is highly likely that you are incorrectly judging a definite situation based on relying on an unrealistic fear. Considering the aforementioned, in order for an act to evaluate the exact specifics of the situation they are dealing with, they should develop the ability to decide whether or not a certain fear is related to an unrealistic subconscious fear that they might have. The artist should always be capable of acknowledging that certain fears are not realistic and helpful; as a matter of fact, the aforementioned can massively damage the development of a healthy professional mentality, as the unrealistic fears encourage negative influences, such as misinterpreting crucial situations that one might find themselves in. Obfuscating the difference in the essence between the unrealistic fear and the intuition can lead to a person subconsciously starting to dent their sense of reality in a highly negative direction, which will ultimately prevent them from taking advantage of choices and opportunities to expand positively their career and life in general. Hence, it is essential for an act to be able to carefully balance the accountability of the effect that fears and intuition can have on one's career. Artists must stand firm against the possibility of developing a long-term fear based on previous particular experiences or moments that can negatively direct their actions, as the experience acquired from unfortunate past events act on your thoughts, not on your intuition. Failing to establish a stable mental protection against such tendencies, the artist can find themselves in a situation where their fears and prejudices can be an obstacle for achieving personal and professional growth of any sort.

CHAPTER 12

Appreciate Your Platform and Always Stay True to Your Personality

Music gives a soul to the universe, wings to the mind, flight to the imagination and life to everything.

—Plato

At the end of the day—as important and crucial as it is to achieve sustainable career through satisfying the market needs of this business—achieving this goal with a product that possesses strong artistic value is the most essential and vital thing that every artist should be aiming to accomplish.

Understanding and completely respecting the tendency that success now-adays means strong and calculated business performance is a necessity; however, the main purpose of the music should be always clear—creating a positive impact, sharing a meaningful message, and changing the world and the lives of the people seeking support through art.

Devotion and Tenacity

It is barely possible for an up-and-coming act to grasp the perception of what overwhelming amount of frustration, disappointment, anxiety, and despair would be experienced throughout the process of establishing a career in the music industry. Expectations will not be met, people will let you down, and would like to see you fail; you will have to learn to cope with the frustration of failing people's ideals, you will find yourself in intense and stressful situations, and you will be the object of judgmental and negative comments. You will receive no support and no one would respect your ideas, desires, thoughts, and quests. The bigger and more successful you get, the more people would like to see you fail and hurt as well. You will be exposed to personal attacks, insults, and disrespectful behavior from people who would like to—plain and simple—make you feel bad about your own accomplishments, achievements, and personality in order to justify their own perceptions and life choices. A point that many people outside of the music business very unreasonably neglect or are not even aware of when it comes to the obstacles that a musician should tackle throughout the process of establishing an activity in the entertainment business is the social one. Pursuing a successful career in the music industry and following your passion and desires nowadays is a task that puts a very overwhelming amount of pressure and stress on talented individuals who are brave enough to follow their personal ambitions. Not complying to the common society standards and expectations, not being able or willing to fulfill people's perceptions of success, and battling the negative prejudices that a vast majority of the personalities around all of us have regarding developing a profile in the music business can be very damaging for the mental state of a person, and only people who are experiencing this cycle personally can fully understand the incredible amount of sacrifices that should be made from a personal point of view in the process of determining a successful career path in music. The amount of stress faced during the experience of investing significant time, efforts, and finances in pursuing the development of a sustainable profile in the music sphere could be incredibly overwhelming. Naturally, the feeling of being alienated by the different notions of successful life expressed and utilized by the majority of society's participants presents an emotional stage that is very hard to overcome. But every music enthusiast should be aware of the fact that there is a certain timeline that should be followed by professionals interested in dedicating their time to generating positive results in the music business, which is very different in its essence than the pattern followed by the rest of the people around us. It is always hard in the beginning, so just keep pushing and keep working hard, and do not forget your goals and where you want to be. There will be times when things will not happen your way and your actions will not be justified. In such situations, you just have to continue moving forward. It is understandable to get discouraged when your peers are securing stable jobs, forming families, and fulfilling the requirements and the expectations forwarded to them by the society, while you are being perceived as a failure by not being able to contribute to the same standards. It is normal to lose faith in your talents and choices once you see that your career progress is not generating the same amount of positive results as you wished or as required. And this is the exact reason why you should be aware of the advantages and the features that your platform as an artist possesses and be fully capable of taking advantage of them in the process of developing and popularizing your activity and improving the results that you are producing. You are in a position to influence people's perceptions about who you are and make them appreciate and seek the exact product that you are offering. You can shape and form your audience's expectations toward your career and plant the requirements in their minds that prompt them to think about your activity by constructing a stable appearance and behavior as an artist, emphasizing on certain aspects of your profession and your strongest traits as a brand. Adding value to a specific characteristic of your activity and bringing attention to it will make the people around you to add value to it as well. It is all a matter of perspective. If you want to be a winner and be perceived as such, you have to first perceive yourself as one and act accordingly.

Influence

At some point, you should be well-aware of how your talent, work, and appearance reflect on the people around you and consider the significance that your activity has. An artist should embrace the influence that they have and be culpable for their actions and the fact that they are not representing just themselves, but a whole community, the business sphere, and all of the respective participants in them. Aim to be respectable. You have voice that can form a generation. Potentially, you can have the platform to encourage and endorse your views and opinions to other people. This is a fantastic opportunity that should be treated very carefully, however. As an influencer, you should be aware of the concept that your actions do not only have effect on your life but reflect on other people as well, as your talent and productivity can have strong effect on the people who choose to be immersed into your art to a level where it can modify and shape certain characteristic features in them, especially in terms of the participants in the music community who possess specific personality traits and are capable of understanding and fully appreciating the abundant potential that music as an art form possesses. Therefore, every musician should know that it is very hard for a standard listener to distinguish the artist from the personality; hence, in many cases, what you do as a person would reflect on your professional career and the vice versa—your career choices would be associated with your personal life. Fundamentally, you sacrifice your own well-being, comfort, and happiness in order to provide them to the people across the world who need a positive influence and support in their respective lives. Appreciate what you do. Love it. Crave it. Always cherish, appreciate, and value the gift that you have been blessed with. You should understand that being in the position of possessing capabilities to use your personal qualities and emotions in the process of creating something in a conventional form that other people can perceive and relate to is a talent that can bring an enormous amount of joy, satisfaction, and pleasure, which are completely unknown and unfamiliar for the majority of the people in the world. The sort of emotions that an artist is able to experience and subsist is amazingly remarkable and unique; therefore, a musician should always aim to recognize the absolute aptitude that an artist has been fortunate enough to possess. Regardless of what you think, what other people tell you, or whatever you achieve eventually, your experience and activity in the music field will be the source of the best, most joyful, and rewarding emotions and times, which you will ever encounter in your life and the only time when you, as a person, will feel absolutely complete, useful, and in harmony with yourself. Wherever you are in life, only music and being able to enjoy the visceral satisfaction that it can give you would be able to bring you the absolutely maximum, sustainable, and long-term happiness that you desire and need in order to feel complete.

Always be yourself and do not be afraid to stay true to your talents, your own style, and way of thinking and doing things. Never forget why you started in the first place. This will help you to stay humble and keep your eyes on the prize. Always respect, cherish, and appreciate the opportunities that your career is providing you with and aim to see the forest through the trees because everything that you are going through and experiencing due to your involvement in the music culture is for a reason. Stay true to your personality and be honest about who you are, because there is nothing worse than people and professionals who are trying to present themselves as the total opposites of their true identity. Let yourself and your character dictate who you are as an artist and what your role is. Do not worry about what other people are thinking or doing; just do what you feel is your true calling and not what you think other people's opinions on the matter are. Do something you love, invest yourself in it, and you will find the satisfaction of committing yourself to your true and genuine purpose, as this would mark the discovery of your existential success, which is the accomplishment that must always guide you through your life.

Bibliography

Allen, P. n.d. *Artist Management for the Music Business*. Waltham, MA: Focal Press.

Bradford, C. 2006. *Artist Management Outloud: The Music Industry Made Crystal Clear*. Wise Publications.

Cann, S. 2009. *Rocking Your Music Business*. Boston, MA: Course Technology, Cengage Learning.

Fink, M. 1989. *Inside the Music Business*. New York, NY: Schirmer Books.

Frascogna, X.M., and H. Lee Hetherington. 2004. *This Business of Artist Management*. New York, NY: Watson-Guptill Publications.

Jamieson, K., and P. Hyland. 2006. "Good Intuition or Fear and Uncertainty: The Effects of Bias on Information Systems Selection Decisions". *Informing Science: The International Journal of an Emerging Transdiscipline* 9, pp. 49–69.

Kemp, C. 2008. *Music Industry Management and Promotion*. Huntingdon: Elm Publications.

Krasilovsky, M.W., S. Shemel, J.M. Gross, and J. Feinstein. 2007. *This Business of Music*. New York, NY: Billboard Books.

Moore, S. 2005. *The Truth about the Music Business*. Boston, MA: Thomson Course Technology PTI.

Morrow, G. 2018. *Artist Management*. Milton: Routledge.

This Game of Artist Management. 1994. New York, NY: A Co. called W.

About the Author

Hristo Penchev is the founder and owner of UAC Management, an independent music management company established in the United Kingdom, author, entrepreneur, philanthropist, an official TEDx lecturer, and a figure with a proven media profile, certified by multiple appearances on numerous traditional and digital media outlets, Hristo Penchev is an industry professional with significant experience in the different spheres of the music business. This experience results from an ongoing and continuous diversified operational activity with a noticeable success rate, including collaborations with a variety of high-level entertainment business participants. Hristo Penchev specializes in artist development, PR, branding, traditional and digital marketing, career strategizing, audience targeting, monetization, media networking, and every other aspect of the process of development and improvement of an artist's career, fundamentally providing guidance for the achievement of both personal and professional success in the current complex landscape of the music industry.

Index

OTHER FORTHCOMING TITLES IN SPORTS AND ENTERTAINMENT MANAGEMENT AND MARKETING

Lynn Kahle, *Editor*

- *Great Coaching and Your Bottom Line: How Good Coaching Leads to Superior Business Performance* by Marijan Hizak
- *Introduction to Sports Marketing: Marketing Through Sports* by Sanjeev Tripathi
- *Introduction to Sports Marketing: Marketing of Sports* by Sanjeev Tripathi
- *Marketing Movies Today: How Studios Are Leveraging Social Media to Promote Feature Films* by Karlin Reiter
- *I Pledge Allegiance to the Team: Implications of Fan Loyalty and Sports Rivalry* by Vassilis Dalakas

Announcing the Business Expert Press Digital Library

Concise e-books business students need for classroom and research

This book can also be purchased in an e-book collection by your library as

- a one-time purchase,
- that is owned forever,
- allows for simultaneous readers,
- has no restrictions on printing, and
- can be downloaded as PDFs from within the library community.

Our digital library collections are a great solution to beat the rising cost of textbooks. E-books can be loaded into their course management systems or onto student's e-book readers.

The **Business Expert Press** digital libraries are very affordable, with no obligation to buy in future years. For more information, please visit **www.businessexpertpress.com/librarians**. To set up a trial in the United States, please email **sales@businessexpertpress.com**.

-compliance